"Michael Glerup has devoted himself to making ........... riches of the early Christian writers, and this thin volume continues this life work. The informative introduction sets us up to thoughtfully appreciate this attractive and readable translation of a remarkable church leader, theologian and spiritual writer."

JAMES C. WILHOIT, PH.D., professor at Wheaton College
and coauthor of *Discovering Lectio Divina*

"I am a great fan of the church of the first four centuries—the church known by the outside culture for how it loved well. Michael Glerup is a trusted scholar who knows how to mine the wisdom and practices of the patriarchs and matriarchs of the early church to make these treasures accessible for twenty-first-century Christians."

GARY W. MOON, M.DIV., PH.D., executive director of the
Dallas Willard Center at Westmont College

"This book was a delight to read! I felt like Gregory of Nyssa was right here in my own sanctuary, preaching to me. Dr. Glerup's wonderful paraphrase has St. Gregory speaking of hedge-fund managers, supermodels, Ponzi schemes and more as he opens the Beatitudes for us. The introduction and the sidebars provide valuable background and suggestions for application. The discussion questions help me to review, consider and live what I had read. But more than simply the form of this book, I delighted in its message, an attractive invitation to enjoy the blessed riches that are available to those who follow the way of Christ."

EVAN B. HOWARD, director of Spirituality Shoppe and author
of *The Brazos Introduction to Christian Spirituality*

"A paraphrase is tricky business. Too much freedom leads to the loss of the original text's meaning. Too little freedom fails to build a bridge into the world of a modern reader. Michael Glerup's paraphrase avoids these dangers and warmly welcomes modern North Americans into the active mind and lively heart of one of the great church fathers."

CHRISTOPHER A. HALL, chancellor of Eastern University

"Many Christians in history embraced treasured ideas that we today easily miss. Gregory of Nyssa thought these 'big thoughts,' and Michael Glerup helps us embrace them, too."

JAN JOHNSON, author of *Abundant Spirituality*

CLASSICS
*in Spiritual Formation*

# GREGORY OF NYSSA

SERMONS ON
THE BEATITUDES

*A Paraphrase by*

## MICHAEL GLERUP

*Foreword by* JONATHAN WILSON-HARTGROVE

IVP Books

An imprint of InterVarsity Press
Downers Grove, Illinois

*InterVarsity Press*
*P.O. Box 1400, Downers Grove, IL 60515-1426*
*World Wide Web: www.ivpress.com*
*E-mail: email@ivpress.com*

*InterVarsity Press® is the book-publishing division of InterVarsity Christian Fellowship/USA®, a movement of students and faculty active on campus at hundreds of universities, colleges and schools of nursing in the United States of America, and a member movement of the International Fellowship of Evangelical Students. For information about local and regional activities, write Public Relations Dept., InterVarsity Christian Fellowship/USA, 6400 Schroeder Rd., P.O. Box 7895, Madison, WI 53707-7895, or visit the IVCF website at <www.intervarsity.org>.*

*Cover design: Cindy Kiple*
*Interior design: Beth Hagenberg*
*Cover images: Thinkstock/Getty Images*
*Interior image: Wikimedia Commons*

*ISBN 978-0-8308-3591-1*

*Printed in the United States of America* ∞

**Library of Congress Cataloging-in-Publication Data**

*Gregory, of Nyssa, Saint, ca. 335-ca. 394.*
 *[De Beatitudinibus. English]*
 *Sermons on the Beatitudes / Gregory of Nyssa ; [edited by] Michael Glerup.*
    *p.cm. — (Classics in spiritual formation)*
 *Includes bibliographical references (p.     ).*
 *ISBN 978-0-8308-3591-1 (pbk. : alk. paper)*
 *1. Beatitudes—Sermons—Sermons 2. Gregory, of Nyssa, Saint, ca. 335-ca. 394—Sermons. 3. Gregory, of Nyssa, Saint, ca. 335-ca. 394. I. Glerup, Michael. II. Title.*
  *BT382.G7413 2012*
  *226.9'306—dc23*

*2012005243*

| P | 18 | 17 | 16 | 15 | 14 | 13 | 12 | 11 | 10 | 9 | 8 | 7 | 6 | 5 | 4 | 3 | 2 | 1 |
|---|----|----|----|----|----|----|----|----|----|---|---|---|---|---|---|---|---|---|
| Y | 27 | 26 | 25 | 24 | 23 | 22 | 21 | 20 | 19 | 18 | 17 | 16 | 15 | 14 | 13 | 12 |

# CONTENTS

# Foreword

When prospective college students or presidential candidates are interviewed, they are occasionally asked a question that is supposed to open a window into their character and aspirations: "If you could have dinner with one person from history, who would it be?" It's a way of asking, "Who is your hero?" or "Who would you most like to learn from?" In many ways, it's a very good question. But it does have its practical challenges. Aside from the straightforward problem that most of the prime candidates for this dinner invitation are dead, there is also this: If, somehow, you could bring them back—or if, for that matter, you could travel through time to sit at their table—how would you understand one another? How, that is, could I as a twenty-first-century English speaker carry on a conversation over dinner with the Aramaic-speaking Jesus of Nazareth or the Latin-speaking Augustine of Hippo? Even if, given years to prepare, I was able to learn the language of my ancient hero, how long would it take us to become familiar enough with one another's contexts to even have a conversation? I know it might seem a little nit-picky, but what I'm getting at is this: if I could have dinner with one person from history, I'm not sure the conversation would go very far. There is, after all, more than time and death that stand between us and those who've gone before.

And yet, despite this great gap, Christians have always tried to listen to people from our history. For 2,000 years, we have remembered the saints. While the fractures of church schisms have dulled our memories of some saints, and while the emphasis on experience in the present has downplayed the role of saints in American evangelicalism, remembrance of the saints has never entirely gone away. This has something to do, I think, with the fact that we are the inheritors of a living tradition. As mysterious and hard to explain as that may be, we have the conviction that those who are dead are not gone. In Christ, they wait with us for that great getting-up morning when, as Scripture reminds us, "the dead in Christ shall rise first." To consider the gift of the communion of saints is to come face to face with the fact that we do, in fact, have dinner with saints from history all the time. We call this meal "the Lord's Supper." It is, as our pastors often remind us, a concrete sign of the unity of the church—"one Lord, one faith, one baptism." We are the one body that we eat. But the "we" here is not just those of us who gather in the same building, the same congregation. It is the "we" of the global body of Christ. And it is the "we" of the church across time. Though we might not be in the habit of remembering this, every Lord's Supper is an opportunity to sit down to dinner with Gregory of Nyssa and Teresa of Ávila, Martin Luther and Fanny Crosby. It's an incredible thing, really. But the miracle of this encounter doesn't guarantee that we'll be able to understand one another. To listen to those who've gone before us, we need help.

All of this to say, if I'm going to have dinner with Gregory of Nyssa—which I have, in a very real sense, enjoyed doing this week—I'm not going alone. I'm bringing Michael Glerup with me. Fact is, Michael has done the homework I haven't. He's taken the time to learn Gregory's Greek, to listen carefully to his context, to pay attention not only to the words he wrote but also to what those words signified in Gregory's fourth-century context. But Michael also lives with me in twenty-first-century America. He reads the same newspapers I do. From what I can tell, he's even watched cable TV. As such, he has the ability to mediate between Gregory's world and my own. This book is a paraphrase of sermons that Gregory preached some 1,700 years ago. In a day when many wonder whether the sermons they hear on a given Sunday have anything to say to their lives, it may seem like a stretch to think about opening yourself to these words. But I'm glad to have this chance to say that I think you should. I think you should because Michael has done an excellent job of paraphrasing Gregory. And because he has, this book will help you to see how well Gregory paraphrased Jesus. And because the body of Christ is a living tradition, I trust that this will help you to become a living paraphrase of the good news in the place where you are. From where I sit, nothing could be more important.

JONATHAN WILSON-HARTRGROVE
3rd Week of Lent, 2012

# INTRODUCTION

Gregory of Nyssa, the little brother of the great bishop of Caesarea, Basil, and friend of the brilliant theologian Gregory of Nazianzus, was the youngest of the influential Cappadocian fathers. In the fourth century, these three were caught up in the great theological debates on the full divinity of Jesus Christ and the doctrine of the Trinity. Their insistence that God is three persons—Father, Son, Holy Spirit—in unity in the face of mounting political pressure won them deep respect in the eyes of the faithful. Today they are acknowledged as the great defenders of trinitarian Christianity.

Today, it is unusual for a theologian to write works on spirituality or ethics, and likewise it is unusual for someone interested in spirituality to compose complicated works in philosophy and theology, but this was not the case in the early church. In fact, many of the great theologians of the ancient church, like Augustine, authored important works on Christian spirituality and morality. Gregory's spiritual writings were thoughtful works of theology and integrated both contemplation and action.

Similar to the actor Alec Baldwin, who after the hugely successful action thriller *The Hunt for Red October* fell out of public view until he landed a role on the television sitcom *30 Rock*, so Gregory's popularity diminished until recently. Although Gregory was known primarily as a philosophical theologian, recently his spiritual writings have enjoyed a resurgence in popularity.

## BACKGROUND

Gregory of Nyssa was born about 335 C.E. in Cappadocia, a mountainous region of northeastern Turkey.[1] Gregory came from a family of ten children, five boys and five girls. Gregory's father died when he was young. The family was distinguished and wealthy, Christian and cultivated. Gregory's older brother

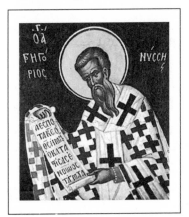

Basil enjoyed an extensive university education under the best-known teachers of his day, but Gregory did not attend university. His education was entirely dependent on Basil and on his sister Macrina. It is clear from his literary works that he read widely in Hellenistic literature, philosophy and science. He inherited much of his thought from the great biblical scholars of Alexandria, Egypt—the third-century Christian Origen and a Jewish philosopher and contemporary of Jesus, Philo. Many themes that he would later develop in his writings were ideas he learned from Basil and Macrina. Gregory exhibited more sympathy to the thought world of his day than did Basil. Whereas Basil was

---

[1]Anthony Meredith, *Gregory of Nyssa* (New York: Routledge, 1999), p. 1.

uneasy with the pointlessness of much contemporary education, Gregory was not.

Gregory's love of learning continued even after he had completed his formal education. He sought wisdom wherever he could find it. At the Council of Constantinople, Gregory had the opportunity to learn from Basil of Ancyra, a trained physician. Basil of Ancyra's lecture on the best medical practices of his day later were incorporated into Gregory's spiritual theology and used frequently to illustrate points of spiritual formation.

In the 350s, Gregory's family embarked on a strict lifestyle of Christian prayer and fasting similar to that practiced in monasteries. Gregory willingly joined his family in these practices, though later he would abandon their way of life. Around 360, Gregory was baptized and ordained a lector, or the person assigned to read the Bible text, other than the Gospel, at the various worship services. In many cases, ordination as a lector served as a probationary or interim position for those wanting to enter into full-time ministry, but this was not so in Gregory's case. He preferred to become a professor of rhetoric.

Public education in Gregory's day was grounded in the Greek classics of literature and philosophy. Many Christian teachers, to the dismay of their pagan contemporaries, modified, adapted and reinterpreted these classics in light of the resurrected Christ. Pagan resentment came to a head during the reign of Julian (361–363), the last of the openly pagan emperors. Julian insisted that only professing pagans should be allowed to teach the classics of Greece. As a result, Christian professors were barred from making a living doing the work they deeply loved. It was after this period of persecution that Gregory most likely became a teacher. His timing of abandoning the ministry for a secular career was viewed with concern by his friends and family. Famously, his choice of profession attracted the rebuke of

Gregory of Nazianzus, who argued that Gregory in his "drunkenness" had abandoned the study of the Bible preferring to gain fame as a professor rather than a Christian. Though later in life Gregory appreciated his friend's censure, at the time it seemed to have no effect. Gregory continued teaching in Caesarea until he became bishop.

Not long after, Gregory married, a choice he would later regret. Though not clearly stated in any of his writings, it appears that Gregory's bride died soon after they were married. After her death, he remained in Caesarea, where he continued to gain respect as a professor. Two watershed events occurred after 370: the death of his mother, Emmelia, and the election of his brother Basil as the bishop of Caesarea. In 372, Basil appointed Gregory bishop of Nyssa, a small and insignificant town in what is now south-central Turkey. Gregory's appointment was political: Basil wished to keep strategic towns under the influence of orthodox bishops. This was not a plum job and not something Gregory agreed to eagerly. Once he did accede to Basil's decision, he pursued his task wholeheartedly. Unlike Gregory of Nazianzus, also appointed against his will, Gregory did not maintain a grudge against his brother. From what little evidence we have on this period of his life, it does seem that Gregory was well liked by his congregation. Though no date was assigned by Gregory when he composed his *Sermons on the Beatitudes*, most scholars believe that they were likely composed during this period.

Gregory's lack of administrative skills and nimbleness in church politics made his tenure as bishop unsuccessful and short-lived. On a false charge of financial mismanagement Arian opposition forced Gregory into exile in 376, where he stayed until the pro-Nicene emperor Theodosius I replaced the emperor Valens (378). Though the facts are not entirely clear, Gregory most likely headed south from Nyssa to take up residence in a small monastery. With his administrative skills chastened, he immersed himself in the study of Scripture and prayer. Perhaps during this period of Scripture study he produced his *Commentary on the Inscriptions of the Psalms* and *On Ecclesiastes*, both important exegetical works.

Soon after Gregory returned from exile, his brother Basil died. This was the beginning of an intense period of activity for Gregory. Assuming the responsibility of his brother's defense of the faith, Gregory took a more active role in doctrinal and theological exposition of the faith. It was during this period that Gregory played a substantial role in the pivotal Council of Constantinople, where the Nicene faith prevailed. After the council, Emperor Theodosius recognized Gregory as a key spokesperson for the orthodox faith. His newfound recognition was further confirmed when he was asked to give the sermon at the funerals for Princess Pulcheria and Empress Flacilla. Throughout much of the 380s, Gregory played a prominent role in church debates and theological education.

Gregory retired from his church duties and left Constantinople around 387. Many of Gregory's most important spiritual works belong to this last period of his life. These classics in Christian spirituality were the fruit of years of study of the Bible, great theological writers and the ancient Greek classics. These were the mature works of a man who not only knew about God but also spent years walking with him. As the Kennedys were to American politics, so Gregory's family was to Christian theological and spiritual education. Gregory inherited a rich tradition of spiritual practice and wisdom from Macrina and Basil. Grateful that they passed along their spiritual wisdom to him, he also felt a deep responsibility to hand down this wisdom to later generations, particularly the monastic communities fostered by Basil.

Gregory passed along his spiritual wisdom primarily through two distinct written forms: short spiritual treatises and biblical commentaries. His most popular spiritual works were in the form of the latter. *Homilies on the Song of Songs* and *Life of Moses*, his most well-known works, as well as his *Sermons on the Beatitudes*, are works of biblical interpretation.

Gregory's name appears on a list of participants at a meeting held in Constantinople in 394. This is the last public record of Gregory. It is believed he died soon afterward.

## THE CONTEXT OF THE SERMONS ON THE BEATITUDES

Prayer and the study of Scripture were both important aspects of Gregory's spiritual life. One biblical book in particular shaped his practices more than any other: the book of Psalms. The Psalms were the most frequently used portions of Scripture in the early church. They were often quoted in the New Testament, and they were the foundation of the churches' daily prayer life. Psalms were recited regularly as part of the practice of daily prayer. In addition to his regular use of the Psalms in his devotions, Gregory also wrote a commentary on the inscriptions (titles) of the Psalms. His goal was to give a general description of the overall aim of the Psalms, for he believed that one must first understand the purpose of the Psalms as a whole before one could interpret the individual psalms. Gregory found that the first word of the first psalm—blessedness—provided the answer to the purpose of the Psalms.

Comparing Psalm 1:1 with the Beatitudes, we see that there are some similarities. The opening verse of the Psalms may be divided into two parts. The first component is *blessed is the man*. Second, we are told the character of the blessed. In this instance, the blessed do not follow evil advice but rather take to heart the wisdom of the Bible. The Beatitudes, like the first verse of Psalm 1, begin with the *blessed*. Likewise, in the second part we are told the character of the blessed, but in this instance it is the poor in spirit, the meek, the pure in heart, the peacemakers, and so on. But the Beatitudes add a third part, and this is usually the focus of Gregory's sermons. The third part states what a person would acquire if he or she became blessed. The blessed will experience the kingdom of heaven. The blessed will be comforted and know themselves as children of God. The blessed will see God, that is, know God in their hearts.

If true blessedness is found in God, then we are not surprised to see that each of these beatitudes is intimately connected to Christ. Christ is the blessed. Christ is meek and merciful. He is the peacemaker. He is justice. He hungered and thirsted for righteousness and suffered for it. He is the firstborn Son of God before all creation. He is the only one who has seen God. Yet, if we have seen him, we have seen the Father. Christ is both the object and the reward of the blessed life. In each sermon, Gregory discusses some aspect of imitating Christ and how this relates to the hoped-for reward.

In his discussion of the Psalms, Gregory argues that the Psalms not only teach us the goal of life but also instruct us on the steps we must take to enter into this blessed life. The first step is to separate ourselves from evil. When we turn our back on evil, we also turn toward that which is better. The second step is to focus our attention on the things of God that are revealed in Scripture. This produces in us not only a desire for good but also the capacity for what is better. The third step is to achieve likeness to God.

This three-stage process of the spiritual life structures Gregory's sermons. In the introduction to the sermon, through examples, Gregory usually compares and contrasts a life enticed by evil and a life lived for God. The side-by-side comparison effectively demonstrates that the life of virtue results in deep joy and therefore is worthy of our best effort. Yet, even though a person decides to pursue a life of virtue, that person still lacks the training to see clearly how life should be lived to its fullest. The next section of the sermon, illustrated with Scripture and examples, provides the listener a deeper understanding of the ways of God. Gregory concludes each sermon on what we will gain from this way of living and how we will take on the likeness of Christ.

Progress in the spiritual life is important for understanding the individual sermons and the sermons as a whole. For Gregory, the Beatitudes are not arbitrarily arranged; they are arranged for ascent. Each beatitude is like a rung on the ladder that leads to heaven or Christlikeness. Gregory's interpretation doesn't always easily fit with the straightforward meaning of the individual verses, so sometimes he is required to resort to some creative interpretive techniques to resolve the problem (see Sermon 2: the reward of land comes after the reward of heaven).

## SPIRITUALITY

InterVarsity Press's Classics in Spiritual Formation series brings the classics of Christian spirituality to contemporary Christians through paraphrases in colloquial English. This volume was chosen for its relevance to contemporary spiritual life.

Gregory has a strong sense of God's transcendence and the infinity of God. As a result, he consistently highlights the importance of trust, love, adoration and obedience to God. He also cautions believers not to think that their words describe God fully or with complete accuracy. Because of God's infinity our words or mental images will always fall short of the actuality of God. This does not indicate that we know nothing or almost nothing about God. Rather, it suggests that our talk about God should be tempered by humility.

God is incomprehensible in God's nature but remains accessible to humans through the inner workings of the soul. God may be known through a way of life that develops the interior attitude and characteristics of Christ. Christ is good, merciful and just, so when we practice justice or develop an interior disposition of mercy, we know God. Gregory writes, "If therefore these good things can be found in you then indeed God is in you . . . and you are able to perceive what is invisible to those not purified."

Gregory steadfastly believed that what we do in life matters. Our choices count. We can participate in our formation. Following the tradition of Eastern Christianity, Gregory understood the Christian life as collaboration between the grace of the Holy Spirit and human effort. Many modern Christians make the mistake of thinking that putting effort into the Christian life is the equivalent of earning merit or God's favor. Consequently, many think putting effort toward their spiritual maturity undermines the important Reformation doctrine that we are justified by faith. But justification by faith opposes earning God's favor, not our efforts to become like Christ.

Rather than emphasize the contrast between effort and earning, Gregory stressed the distinction between the love for the Father and love of the world. As the epistle writer states, "For everything in the world—the lust of the flesh, the lust of the eyes, the pride of life—comes not from the Father but from the world" (see 1 Jn 2:16 NIV). For Gregory, laziness, indulgence and callous indifference to the suffering of others characterize the lives of those who love the world. On the other hand, the life of a follower of Christ is characterized by a fierce but steady courage. Easy is the life of the world until it collapses under the weight of its indulgence. Demanding is the path that leads through the narrow gate of Christlikeness into the adventure and the beauty of the love of God.

The final observation concerning Gregory's spirituality is that progress in the spiritual life and knowledge of God will continue indefinitely. Human spiritual progress does not have a limit because the desire of our heart, the Trinity, is limitless. As a result, when we experience God in prayer, we experience the paradox of the deep satisfaction of God's presence; yet, at the same time, we experience God's absence because God remains constantly beyond us. In the life to come we will continue to grow in our knowledge and love of God. Our knowledge of God's love will, paradoxically, grow without the awareness of less.

Gregory's work will feed the spiritual lives of contemporary readers, especially in his unwillingness to separate

- action from contemplation
- compassion from prayer
- "just living" from Scripture study

This text is worth reading slowly and reflectively with attention to the sidebars relating to spiritual formation and the questions at the back of the book. May it enrich your spiritual life.

SERMON

1

Blessed are the poor in spirit,

for theirs is the kingdom of heaven.

*You're blessed when you're at the end of your rope. With less of you there is more of God and his rule.*

When Jesus saw his ministry drawing big crowds, he climbed a hillside. Those who were apprenticed to him, the committed, climbed with him. Arriving at a quiet place, he sat down and taught his climbing companions. This is what he said: "You're blessed when you're at the end of your rope. With less of you there is more of God and his rule."

Who here is an apprentice of the Word such that he is willing to climb up the hillside from the valley of shallow living to the spiritual mountain of breathtaking prayerfulness? This mountain rises above the shadows shed by the rolling hills of

depravity and is fully immersed by the glow of the true light.
From the vantage point of the summit, what was invisible
from below is now seen in the crystal-clear air of truth. Now
the Word of God himself points out to his fellow mountain-
eer the various points that can be seen only from higher ele-
vations. With his index finger he figuratively directs our eyes
to the kingdom of the heavens, then to the inheritance of the
land above, then to mercy and justice and reassurance. Next
he directs our gaze to our likeness with God and finally to
the reward of persecution, that is, to become a friend of God.
All these spiritual truths and more are identified for us by
Jesus the Word as we take in the panoramic view through the
eyes of hope.

As we watch the Lord climb up the mountain let us remember
what was written in Isaiah: "Come, let's climb God's Mountain
. . . [where God will] show us the way he works so we can live
the way we're made" (Is 2:3). If our soul, made fearful by sin,
questions our stamina to make the climb, let us take heart,
"energiz[ing] the limp hands [and] strengthen[ing] the rubbery
knees" because, as the prophet tells us, God is here and will
make things right (Is 35:3-4). For when we reach the top we will
find Jesus, the one who heals every disease, whether mental,
emotional or physical (Mt 4:23), and fulfills Isaiah's farsighted
prediction: "He took our illnesses, He carried our diseases" (Mt
8:17). So therefore let us scramble up the mountain as fast as we
can make it. And like the prophet Isaiah gazing from the summit of hope we too see the good things that the Word shows to
those who follow him wherever he goes. Likewise may the Word
of God speak to us once more, teaching us those things that are
a blessing to hear, as we dig into the teachings of Jesus.

Blessed, he says, are the poor in spirit, for theirs is the
kingdom of the heavens. Imagine a greedy hedge-fund man-

ager coming by chance on a treasure map that supplied the
exact location of a huge stash of cash. The only problem is
that the treasure's location is difficult to reach, and once there
it will be labor-intensive to obtain. What do you think the
entrepreneur will do? Do you think he will drag his feet because he is discouraged by the difficulties? Do you think,
after doing a cost-benefit analysis, he would decide not to go
for it because it would require hard work on his part? Not a
chance! Instead, he would reach out to his buddies and in-
volve as many as he could in order to lessen the load. He
would make calls to local contractors and secure the services
of day laborers in order to dig up the treasure and move it to
a safe location.

Likewise, brothers and sisters, this gospel passage we are
studying is a map to a huge stash of cash, though its riches are
buried in the obscurity of the biblical passage. Therefore, like
the greedy industrialist but with the desire for the pure gold of
God, let us gather a group of our hard-working friends and together, in prayer, extract God's wisdom hidden in this passage
in order that all of us might equally share in its spiritual wealth.
The nature of spiritual wealth is different from earthly wealth.
Spiritual wealth is not diminished when it is shared with others.
When spiritual wealth is equally shared among co-laborers,
each receives the entire amount. In the distribution of earthly
wealth, which is like a pie, if one person wrongly takes a larger
portion, the portion of the others is reduced. But spiritual
wealth is like our experience of the warmth and brightness of
the sun. No matter how much time we spend in the sun soak-
ing up its rays, it doesn't take away from the experience of another person doing the same thing. The sun's warmth and
brightness are wholly available to all. Since the nature of spiritual wealth is such that all benefit from it, similarly let us fully

cooperate with each other in prayer so that together we can receive the same benefit.

Before we go any further it would be wise of us to first ask how we should define beatitude or blessedness. I understand blessedness to be a state of unconditional happiness and contentment. Sometimes it is easier to learn the meaning of something by comparing it with its opposite, and such is the case with the meaning of blessedness. The opposite of blessedness is extreme unhappiness, which is the undesirable experience of anguish that is the result of unbearable misery. The attitude of a person experiencing blessedness is significantly different from that of the person experiencing misery. Joy and happiness are the characteristics of someone called blessed, whereas grief and distress characterize a person unhappy with his or her circumstances. Yet, if truth be told, the only thing truly blessed is God himself. Whatever we suppose "God-ness" to be, blessedness is that perfect life of good. It is a life of unimaginable good and beauty. It is a life of wisdom, power and grace. It is true light, that is, it is the source of all goodness. It is the most dominant force for good in the universe. It is the sole object of love, which remains unchanged and enjoyed forever as the eternal source of happiness. Yet no matter what we say, our description never seems adequate to the reality of its beauty and goodness. Our earthbound opinions cannot adequately describe its infinite reality. Even if we do manage to go beyond the limits of our intelligence, no verbal expression can communicate our deepest thoughts about God.

Yet God made us "in the image of God." So indirectly we, who are created in the likeness of true blessedness, experience blessedness. Let me give you an example of what I'm trying to say. Take, for instance, the physical beauty of a supermodel captured on the cover of a women's magazine. The real beauty is the supermodel herself. Yet, secondarily, we can attribute that same beauty to the photographic image. Likewise human beings are images of the transcendent blessedness, and similarly as copies we may be said to possess the same beauty when we display the features of blessedness. Unfortunately sin has stained and defaced the image of God in humanity such that we, as humans, no longer image God as we should. Yet, when Christ came with his own cleaning solution, the living water "welling up to eternal life" (Jn 4:14 NIV), the appalling discoloration of sin was washed away and the image of God was restored.

Consider another example, that of a portrait artist. If asked by an amateur to depict beauty he might begin by describing a beautiful face as being composed of bronzed skin, full lips, dark shaped eyebrows, higher cheekbones and a narrow nose, which all together compose a striking profile. Well, in a similar manner the Artist of our soul redraws our inner face in the image of blessedness, by sketching, in this gospel passage, each feature that lures us toward blessedness. So he says at the beginning, "Blessed are the poor in spirit, for theirs is the kingdom of the heavens."

As we approach this particular verse, we must face up to the fact that no matter how wonderful a gift this teaching may be, it will be beneficial only if we know how to apply its meaning to our circumstances. The wisdom of Scripture is like a large pharmacy stocked with a variety of medicines that can be applied to relieve an assortment of ailments. Yet these medicines remain useless to us unless we know how they should be administered and under what conditions. Likewise scriptural wisdom remains ineffective unless we can establish the meaning of the terms employed. So to begin our first question is: What does it mean to be "poor in spirit"?

First, we know from reading Scripture, especially passages

like Matthew 6:19-20, that there are two kinds of wealth, one which is to be desired and one which is to be shunned. The former, the riches of virtue, is a benefit to the soul, whereas the latter, material wealth, is a detriment to the soul because it is tied up with things that sidetrack us from the business of heaven. Therefore, the Lord condemns the hoarding of "treasure down here where it gets eaten by moths and corroded by rust or—worse!—stolen by burglars" (Mt 6:19) and urges us to stash our treasure in heaven, where it is safe from the forces of decay. But does it make literal sense to connect moth, rust and burglars to spiritual wealth? Not really. In fact, I think it best to interpret these corrupting forces spiritually, so as to refer to the corruptor of spiritual treasure, that is, the Evil One.

Now if poverty is contrasted with wealth, then it seems that by way of analogy there are two forms of poverty, one that we should steer clear of and another that is to be called blessed. Consider the person who is deficient in the virtues of self-control, justice, wisdom, sound judgment or other great treasures. Should he not be regarded as miserable and contemptible because he is bankrupt in the things that are of value? Likewise, consider the person bankrupt in things considered evil. She has not hoarded the devil's treasures in the warehouse of her heart but kept her spirit passionate and accordingly stockpiles in herself the absence of evil. Isn't this the type of person whom Jesus, the Word of God, identifies as poor in the sense of blessed, whose reward is the kingdom of the heavens?

But I digress; let us return to the topic of treasure. "Blessed," he says, "are the poor in spirit." In other writings and sermons I've taught that the goal of the really good life is likeness to God. Yet this is difficult to understand and can sound a little New Age-y, because it is impossible for human beings to imitate a God of purity who does not change or experience suffering.

Think about it: doesn't it appear impossible for human beings—trapped in suffering and the emotional ups and downs of
life—to become like the God who exists unchangingly in perfect happiness? Let me summarize the problem: if it is—as the
apostle Paul teaches—that God alone is blessed and that humans share in that blessedness through their likeness to God,
and yet, imitation of God is impossible, then it follows that
blessedness is unattainable for the typical person.

But that doesn't add up. It seems to me that there are some
aspects of God that can be imitated by those who want to follow
Christ. What are they? A good example is voluntary humility,
which I feel is the proper understanding of the phrase "poor in
spirit." The apostle Paul's teaching that "our Lord Jesus Christ,
that though he was rich, yet for your sakes . . . became poor, so
that you through his poverty might become rich" (2 Cor 8:9) is
a good biblical example of what I mean. So, unlike every other
aspect of God's nature, which goes far beyond the limits of our
nature, humility is something that is natural to us. This is especially true when we take into consideration our humble origin
and the uncomfortable fact that when we die, our bodies, which
can be such a source of pride in this life, will one day decom-
pose into garden fertilizer. Consequently, if we imitate God in
what is natural to us, then it can be said we have put on the
blessed form.

But don't think humility is something that can be achieved
easily or without practice! Quite the opposite: humility requires
more practice and effort than any other highly sought-after
character trait. Why? Because humility's opposite—the sin of
pride—is deeply ingrained in our being. As Jesus taught in the
parable of the wheat and tares, we're God's field that has been
lovingly planted with God's good seed, but during the night our
mortal enemy planted the seed of pride. This same seed, pride,

which caused the downfall of the devil, also caused the downfall of the human race in Adam's rebellion. I want to be clear on this issue: There is no evil that so wounds our soul as pride.

Since a sense of superiority is deeply ingrained in almost every human being, our Lord makes this the beginning of his discussion on the blessed life. He expels pride, the primary source of all evil, from our character by encouraging us to live our life like our Lord, the model of blessedness, who by his own free will became poor so that we might realize for ourselves a share of his blessedness. As Paul instructs, "Think of yourselves the way Christ Jesus thought of himself. He had equal status with God but didn't think so much of himself that he had to cling to the advantages of that status no matter what. Not at all. When the time came, he set aside the privileges of deity and took on the status of a slave, became human! Having become human, he stayed human. It was an incredibly humbling process" (Phil 2:5-8). What could be lower for God than to take on the status of a slave? What could be more humbling than for the Ruler of creation to share in our human condition?

Let this sink deep within your spirit: the Ruler of rulers and the Lord of lords freely took on the status of a slave. The universal Judge submitted himself to the judgment of local officials. He who holds the universe in his hands finds no room available at the hostel, so he is laid—out in the cold—in a feeding trough made for farm animals. The unspoiled accepts the pollution of the human condition and journeys through the muck of life to the experience of death. Do you see the standard by which we are to judge our poverty? Life experiences death. The Judge is put on trial. The Ruler of the angelic host allows the executioner to perform his duty. Our Lord says through his actions, "Let this be the standard on which you assess the quality of your humility."

A brief examination of the silly pretensions of human pride might serve us well in our quest to enter into the blessed life, since humility is easily achieved once it is established as the most reasonable way to live. Like a physician who doesn't just treat the symptoms but eradicates the source of the disease and allows the body to return to health, so we will remove the pompous delusions of arrogance through sound reasoning and thereby make the path of humility easier to travel.

How might we demonstrate the futility of pride? How better than by taking an honest look at human nature? Let's begin, what is a human being? There are a number of ways of answering this question. Some answers, which focus on the best qualities of humanity, are more flattering, and others not so. Yet, even someone who recognizes the nobility of every person must also consider the manner in which the author of Genesis describes our common origin—God formed the first human beings from clay. Yes, the same material that is used to make bricks! It is difficult to justify the pretensions of the rich and famous when you realize they share a common ancestry with a pizza stone. (Some might argue they were generated not from clay but from the sexual act of their parents—but be careful if you dig up your family history. You might find you are the product of an inappropriate sexual relationship [see Lev 18:6-18]—a source of family dishonor. Whatever the case, this is not a subject appropriate for a public forum.)

What about those who are swelled with pride, full of themselves, deluded by images of their own grandeur? Don't they consider the terminal points of human life—of where it begins and where it ends? Most people don't. They usually perceive themselves based on an ideal image formed in their prime. Young men take pride in their handsome appearance, their athletic prowess and their thick head of hair. They retain an air of superiority because they wear the hippest clothes from all the top-name designers; even their shoes ooze self-importance. They focus only on the external. They give credence to those things that fade with time . . . but do they really look at themselves? Of course not! But let's hold up a mirror so that we can get an accurate picture of who we are.

Have you ever seen news images of a mass gravesite from some natural disaster or genocidal rampage? Bones and limbs are carelessly strewn about. Skulls with their empty eye sockets stare blankly into the distance. If you have, then you have seen yourself. Gone from these bones is the captivating image of youth. Where are those high cheekbones bronzed by the sun? Or those full lips or sparkling eyes surrounded by thick lashes set under a shaped brow? Or that Fabio-like hair that gently falls to your shoulders? Or those accoutrements of status—clothes, watches, cars, second homes at the beach or

> **Remember Your Death**
>
> *"Remember the day of your death," said the desert father Evagrius. "Remembering your death" was an ancient spiritual practice in the desert and in the monastery. This was not a morbid preoccupation with death but a healthy discipline to understand life in its full context. When we remember that we are going to die, we realize that time is not a limitless resource. The practice reminds us to attach our life to something that will never end. I die. I decay. I'm forgotten. In Christ, though, I live. Humbled, I get to let go of my feeble attempts to make a life and invest in things that will last. I choose to trust in the One who was, who is and who will be.*

on the slopes? Where in these bones do you find all those things that now serve as a source for your self-aggrandizement? Are they not delusions? Or momentary glimpses of a youth that vanish as quickly as they appeared?

Now I don't want to seem to be picking on young people. Their foolishness stems from their lack of perspective, which comes from experience. But what about those in their 70s and whose youth is gone, yet their character is unstable and the disease of pride continues to grow? They tend to be more sophisticated in their ruse by demanding the respect rightful to a person of their stature. They usually justify this thinly veiled form of pride on their position or title and the decision-making authority that goes along with their job. But the disease of pride accompanied them when they were being groomed for the position and was obvious while they occupied the position, and even after it began to fade after years of being out of the office, it could easily be revived with the retelling of a few war stories with former colleagues. Do you see their deception? They justify their pride on the basis of their situation or status, yet, as their situation or status changed, the disease of pride remained constant.

Puffed up by their seeming importance these people consider neither the past nor the future. Instead, puffed up by seeing their names in the headlines, they swell with self-importance, adopting an air of gravitas. They adopt gestures and facial expressions and speak with fabricated sincerity in an attempt to manipulate their audience. Convinced of their own importance, no longer bound to the limits of the ordinary, they overreach. Because their decisions affect a vast segment of society, they begin to believe that, like God, they are masters over life and death, forgetting that it is God who sets the seasons and times for everything. You think they might consider the stories of world leaders such as President John F. Kennedy or Polish President Lech Kaczynski, both of whom died unexpectedly and tragically in office. One day at the table with the most influential leaders in the world, and the next residing in a grave outside the corridors of power.

Yet, how can a person be a master of another when he is not even the master over his own life? He can't. It would be silly to think he could. If a person were on the ball, she would consider the advantage of becoming poor in spirit and look to him who, for our sake, willingly became poor. No longer deceived by their fleeting status, these people would become respecters of all persons, recognizing the equality of all. Then they would be truly blessed because they exchanged a provisional humility for the kingdom of the heavens.

This is not the only interpretation of poverty. A person would be wise to take heed of Jesus' caution to the rich young man to "sell your possessions; give everything to the poor. All your wealth will

> **Servant Leadership**
>
> *Until recently, secular models of leadership, which defined leadership in terms of effectiveness and managerial performance, were seemingly at odds with Christian understandings of leadership, which emphasized character and service. Now many leadership consultants and academics argue that effective organizations require persons with high moral character and service ethic, which develop out of deep spiritual commitments. Gregory's case for humility, based on radical honesty about our humanness, as the basis for servant leadership makes a lot of sense today.*

then be in heaven" (Mt 19:21). This understanding of poverty fits well with the poverty that Jesus called blessed. Further along in the same passage Peter says to Jesus, "We left everything and followed you. What do we get out of it?" I imagine that Jesus very easily could have replied, "Blessed are the poor in spirit, for theirs is the kingdom of heaven" (Mt 5:3 NIV). The poor in spirit, then, are the persons who pawn their bling (material wealth) for an enriched spiritual life; that is, they become poor for the sake of the spirit. . . .

The task for followers of Christ is to take on the things that lift our spirit and let go of, that is, become poor to, the things that drag us down. Psalm 112 provides some good direction on how this is to be accomplished: "They lavish gifts on the poor— A generosity that goes on, and on, and on" (v. 9). The person who gives lavishly will share in him who gave lavishly for our sake. We do not need to be afraid of poverty. Why? Because the Lord, who became poor for us, is the ruler over all of creation. It stands to reason that if you share your life with the least, the last and the lost, modeling your life on Christ, then you will certainly share in his kingdom. "Blessed are the poor in spirit, for theirs is the kingdom of heaven" (NIV). Our prayer is that we will be found worthy of the reign of Christ Jesus, our Lord, to whom be the glory and dominion forever and ever. Amen.

## 2

Blessed are the meek,

for they will inherit the earth.

*You're blessed when you're content with just who you are—no more, no less. That's the moment you find yourselves proud owners of everything that can't be bought.*

The ladder is a practical image for understanding the spiritual life. To climb a ladder, a person steps up on the first rung and then proceeds to the second rung. One step follows another until eventually the person winds up on top of the ladder. It seems to me the Beatitudes are like rungs on a ladder. They are not arbitrarily arranged. They follow a pattern that, if understood correctly, will aid growth into spiritual maturity.

Now if my conviction—the Beatitudes are organized as steps to spiritual maturity—is correct, then we must address one

### Ladder

*Among early Christian writers, a ladder stretching from earth to heaven, similar to the one in Jacob's dream, became a popular image for the journey to spiritual maturity. Most famous was John Climacus's* The Ladder of Divine Ascent. *His ladder had thirty rungs or steps, one for each of the thirty years of Christ's life before his public ministry began. The image of the ladder shaped the imagination of both Eastern and Western Christianity. In the East, it was used frequently in icons. In the icon, John often is depicted at the bottom of the ladder with a scroll pointing to the ladder. At the top of the ladder is Christ reaching out to those who have made the arduous journey. On the right of the ladder are angels encouraging the faithful as they climb; on the left, demons try to pull them down. I like the ladder as an image of the spiritual journey with a slight modification: the ladder as a spiral staircase. Like a ladder, the staircase depicts the journey as a progression toward Christ and maturity. The addition of the spiral reminds us that we will continue to revisit the same family issues, longings and temptations throughout our journey. Returning to these issues does not indicate failure in our journey to maturity. Rather, we reencounter these issues further along the path, a fact that allows these truths learned in the past to deepen.*

glaring problem right away: How can the promise *to inherit the earth* be superior to possessing *the kingdom of the heavens*? Isn't it obvious that the kingdom of the heavens is higher than or superior to inheriting the earth? Doesn't it seem more reasonable to put the earth before heaven, since our progression is upward? The answer is yes if we answer this question from a human perspective but not from a spiritual perspective. The key to a spiritual perspective is the two-tiered portrayal of heaven in the opening chapter of Genesis. Here it teaches that on the second day, God is said to have created a vault (in some translations it is referred to as the "firmament") in heaven to "separate water from water." Below this vault are the "heavens" and the physical earth. Above the vault is the throne of God and the "new earth," which is set aside as an inheritance for those who have lived the Jesus way. Viewed from this perspective it makes sense that the Beatitudes are arranged such that God promises the heavens and then land. From the perspective of our senses, then, the heavens are higher than the earth, but the realm referred to here is beyond sense perception, so our point of view must be recalibrated so that we think in spiritual terms and not just material.

It should not be a surprise, then, that the spiritual realms are referred to as land (or earth). Remember the Lord, out of his love for his creation, became a human being; that is, he adapted himself to our limited understanding. Why? Because we were not able to rise up to him. In the same manner, he communicates spiritual truths using terms and concepts drawn from human experience. He did this in the previous blessing when he referred to the heavens as a kingdom. Do you think Christ intended to communicate that the heavens are like an earthly monarchy? Something similar to the pageantry associated with the royal wedding of Kate and William? Or an impressive pal-

ace throne room adorned with gold and lit by crystal chande-
liers and surrounded by rows of armed palace guards to project
power and importance? No. He spoke in those terms because
the earthly monarchy, at the time, was a symbol of the highest
aspiration of human achievement. If something else existed
that was higher in the minds of his listeners than the kingdom,
he would have surely used that term instead.

The problem is that it is impossible to reveal literally these
spiritual truths that go beyond human knowledge and intellectual capabilities. The apostle Paul makes a similar argument in
his first letter to the Corinthians: "No one's ever seen or heard
anything like this, never so much as imagined anything quite
like it—what God has arranged for those who love him" (1 Cor
2:9). We learn about the blessed life in familiar terms in order
that we get at least a glimpse into this spiritual reality. So don't
get sidetracked by the term "land," though it comes after
heaven, and in so doing be drawn away from the more important spiritual realities. Rather, if you have gained any insight
from the practice of the first beatitude, then focus your attention on the land inherited only by those who have become followers of the Jesus way.

I think King David, inspired by the Spirit, also saw the value
of living the Jesus way. The Scriptures indicate, especially in
relation to his generation, that his life was characterized by
gentleness and forgiveness. By faith he had achieved the things
for which we hope, as shown when he said, "I'm sure now I'll
see God's goodness in the exuberant earth" (Ps 27:13). I do not
think that the prophet refers to this earth as the "land of the
living," since he was aware that the things produced by the
earth will be eventually recycled back into the ecosystem.
Rather, he knows that in the land of the living, death is a dis-
tant memory. It is the land in which its inhabitants do not hang

out at Sin Saloon, or slink along Dead-End Road or go to Smart-Mouth College (see Ps 1:1). Nor is it the land sown with the bad seed by the work of the enemy, and it therefore does not produce thistle and thorns; rather, it is a well-watered land of lush meadows (see Ps 23:2), like the Garden of Eden where the four rivers spring forth and the real Vine cultivated by the God of the cosmos grows (see Jn 15:1), and all the other inspired metaphors that Scripture employs to describe it.

If we prayerfully direct our attention to the land that is higher than the heavens, whose hub is the city of the King—the city that everyone who's in the know talks about (see Ps 87:3)—then we will not be surprised by the ordering of the Beatitudes. In any case, I find it highly unlikely that our present-day earth is offered as a sign of hope to those of us who are still alive at the end time. As Paul says, we "will be caught up with them into the clouds to meet the Master" (1 Thess 4:17). Seriously, why do we need this land anymore, when we hope "to walk on air" with the Lord? For, as Paul states, at that time we "will be caught up with them into the clouds to meet the Master. Oh, we'll be walking on air! And then there will be one huge family reunion with the Master. So reassure one another with these words" (1 Thess 4:17-18).

Let's return to our discussion on the virtue for which the reward is the inheritance of the land. "Blessed are the meek, for they will inherit the earth." What then is meekness? And in what manner is meekness blessed? I would argue that not everything done meekly is to be considered virtuous, especially if you mean by meekness something that is done quietly and leisurely. Surely the meek slacker is not going to win the 400m race, nor is the listless fighter going to win his bout against an aggressive opponent. In fact, Paul encourages us in the race for the prize of salvation, to run hard and fast, that is, "Run to win!" (1 Cor 9:24). Paul kept his "eye on the goal, where God is beckoning us onward—to Jesus," and he was "off and running . . . not turning back" (Phil 3:14). As a fighter, he was light on his feet and kept a close eye on his opponent's onslaught. Speaking metaphorically, Paul had hands of stone. He didn't merely shadow box, but he attacked his opponent; pounding his opponent's body with hard-hitting blows. Do you want a behind-the-scenes look at Paul's fighting technique? Then look at the shiner and the bruises he gave his opponent. Surely you can make out his adversary, who attacked through the fleshly nature and whom he beat back with his spiritual fighting techniques—chastity, fasting, learning patience through hardship and enduring persecution for the sake of Jesus. Paul defeated his enemy by pushing to the front so that his view of the prize in Christ Jesus was not obscured. Paul was one bad dude; he reminds me of David, who chased down his enemies (see Ps 18:36-38).

With so many examples like these scattered throughout the Bible, why does Jesus the Word call meekness a blessing? Again, "Blessed are the meek, for they will inherit the earth." The Word communicates in such a way to make this point: In life and nature there is tendency toward evil that can quickly gain momentum if given the chance. It is the same as a boulder falling from a high ridge. As it bounds down the hillside it gains speed until it is hurtling down at a frightening rate, crushing whatever it hits at the bottom. So, as we can see, there are instances when speed is bad, so it is reasonable that its opposite is blessed. Meekness, then, is the measured and cautious attitude toward these natural tendencies. Our typical disposition is quick to stoke the flames of evil, so in this instance anything that quietly and gently resists is called blessed.

This is not easily understood, so maybe a few examples

from life might illustrate the point better. Every person in making a choice has an opportunity to exert his or her will in either direction—toward virtue or vice. In life we are faced with conflicting impulses: the choice between anger or agape, arrogance or humbleness, cruelty or kindheartedness, jealousy or desiring the best for others. The nature of human life is that we cannot be completely free from these competing impulses. The Lord does not ask us to live our life in such a way that we are completely cut off from these passions because that would be impossible. He does call us to live within our capability for virtue. And gentleness is within our reach. To be gentle is to be blessed.

It would be unworthy of a good and loving God to command us to do something by definition we cannot do. To do so would be like requiring a fish to thrive in the atmosphere or to require birds to live underwater. The Lord, in his loving goodness, adjusts his requirements for us to fit to our present capabilities. So, as we read in this beatitude, the Lord requires us to be unpretentious and gentle in our relationships. He does not require us to be totally free from conflicting emotions, for the latter is wholly beyond our reach and the former is achievable but attained only through years of practice. We are not called to be Spock-like in our demeanor, that is, unmoved by our desires. If this is not so, what would be the benefit of blessings in this life? Are we not motivated by our desire for blessing? The Lord insists that a person is not to be condemned if by chance she feels conflicting emotions or desires; rather, the person to be condemned is the one who has knowingly allowed herself to be dominated by these strong feelings. In many instances these urges rise up in us against our will. Therefore the requirement of virtue is not to let ourselves to be swept away by these impulses but courageously resist them by applying the reasoned

truths of Scripture. Blessed are those who are not easily captivated by the hot-blooded movements of the heart but are
soothed by reason. Like the bridle reins on a fast-charging
horse, reason restrains these negative impulses from carrying
us away into unruliness.

What I'm trying to say here might be better illustrated by
considering the difference between gentleness and anger. Think
of a time when someone cut you off on the road or treated you
rudely or with contempt, and how you could feel your blood
pressure rise, the veins popping out on your forehead as your
spirit rose up to seek vengeance. It's just like in the movie *The
Incredible Hulk*, where suddenly the normally mild-mannered
professor is transformed by anger into a beast. His eyes bloodshot and filled with rage, hair standing on end, voice raspy and
rough with anger, spitting out incoherent words, his whole
body infected with rage. But a person guided by the beatitude,
feeling the anger rise up, would evenly and gently apply God's
reasoning to his wound, allowing its soothing affects to calm
his spirit. Now compare the two. Wouldn't you agree the beastly
figure transformed by rage is to be pitied? And the person
guided by the beatitude who was not distracted by the wrong
done to him—isn't he to be considered blessed?

It seems clear then that Jesus the Word refers to this condition since he prescribes gentleness immediately after humility.
It makes sense that gentleness follows closely after humility;
for it is well known that humility is the womb of gentleness. If
a person frees himself from pride it is highly unlikely that anger
will take hold. Insults and putdowns infuriate the prideful person but not the person practiced in humility. For if people
would stop deceiving themselves long enough to take an honest
look at their life and their condition (their brief lifespan, bodily
excrements and other fluids that come out of the weirdest

places, continual neediness), and, moreover, meditate on their pains, miseries and the various diseases that undermine human integrity, they would begin to see life more clearly. With the eye of the soul purified by honesty, a person gains a better picture of reality and thereby is less likely to be irritated or annoyed by the lack of respect from others.

But if an acquaintance expresses admiration for some reason or another, don't take it too seriously since even the good things that we do are not that great and the character qualities that are praiseworthy are usually not held in high esteem by the world. For to base your self-image or self-esteem on the amount of money in your bank account, the status of your family, your popularity, or other benchmarks by which you judge yourself superior to your neighbor are the things that do damage to your soul. Consequently, it would be the summit of stupidity to choose to damage your soul with such nonsense. This is what it means to be humble: not to take yourself too seriously.

The good news is that when humility is achieved, anger will find no way to do damage to the soul. In the absence of anger, a life of inner calm and contentment is achieved, which is the same thing as meekness or gentleness. And we know that the outcome of such a life is blessedness and the inheritance of the kingdom of heaven in Jesus Christ, to whom be glory and dominion forever and ever. Amen.

SERMON

3

Blessed are those who mourn,
for they will be comforted.

*You're blessed when you feel you've lost what is most dear to you. Only then can you be embraced by the One most dear to you.*

We are making steady progress on our journey to the summit as we pass over the first ridge of poverty of spirit and then up and over meekness, which is higher still. Our able guide, Jesus the Word, leads us higher, directing us to the third ridge in view by way of the Beatitudes. To climb this next pitch we will need to follow the apostle's instruction: "Strip down, start running—and never quit! No extra spiritual fat, no parasitic sins" (Heb 12:1). No longer weighed down by nagging distractions and the unnecessary load of sin on our souls, we can see more clearly the truth that is in front of us.

The question before us today is: What does the saying mean "Blessed are those who mourn, for they will be comforted"? For the sake of argument let's approach this saying from the point of view of those wise in the ways of the world. Surely the worldly-wise must think a statement like this to be outlandish. They would argue, "Surely if those plagued by every kind of misfortune are called blessed, then it follows that those who live a charmed life free from sorrow must be miserable." To further their point they would mockingly describe the dismal condition of street kids and the homeless to provoke contemptuous laughter. They would then go on painting a picture of your worst nightmare: financial ruin, accidents, false imprisonment, abduction in a foreign country; followed by descriptions of exile, confiscation of property and public humiliation. Just to drive home the point they would move on to physical suffering: blindness, paralysis, amputation or physically deforming diseases. In all, they would detail every kind of physical and emotional suffering that might be experienced in this life, thus proving, at least to themselves, the absurdity of saying that the sorrowful are the happy ones.

These small-minded persons, who have little regard for the wisdom of God, will not put us off. We, instead, will do our best to dig deeper into the Scriptures to mine its mysterious wisdom. We hope that through our discussion the difference between the mind concerned with the things of God and the mind that is not will be made plain.

Now there is a sadness that may be appropriately called blessed that correlates to Paul's teaching on the regret that arises out of sins and transgressions. Paul teaches that there are two forms of distress: one that drives people away from God and another that drives people toward God. The effect of the former is a deathbed of regrets while the other produces salvation through godly repentance (see 2 Cor 7:10). If the truth were told, I think that if a person is more sensitive, more reverent, more responsible because of his or her grief over a life lived without God that this distress falls within the definition of blessedness. Think of it this way: If a person suffers from a significant head or back trauma, it is not necessarily a good sign that he cannot feel the prick of a pin on his extremities. But if, through the best medical care available, the patient's toes and feet again experience the pain of the needle prick, it is a source of encouragement for both the doctors and the patient because they know it is a good sign for someone on the road to recovery.

This analogy is consistent with what Paul says about those who have lost touch with God. Disconnected from a life with Christ and befuddled in their thinking, they are no longer alert to the consequences of their actions. But then, like a physician administering a series of remedial treatments, Jesus the Word dispenses warnings of future judgment that pierce the heart with fear of potential consequences. This fear is stoked by hearing biblical imagery associated with future separation from God: unending anguish, ravenous flames, gnashing of teeth, unbounded grief and the isolation of deep darkness. These treatments of "reality" are administered in just the right dose to reduce the swelling and numbness caused by the damage of distorted desires. The patient now aware of the pain of regret caused by a life lived without God is said to be blessed because of the suffering that returned him to health. Paul, in a similar way, ripped on the man sleeping with his stepmother, until he became aware of the sinfulness of his behavior. But once the medicine of Paul's reprimand penetrated the man's callousness, Paul then began to encourage him, as if he was now blessed by regret, in order that he wouldn't drown in his guilt (2 Cor 2:7). I think it is important we always keep this reading of the beati-

## Medicine of Salvation

*Gregory frequently draws from the medical profession to illustrate truths about the spiritual life. Well-informed about the best medical practices of his day, Gregory peppered his sermons with this knowledge to draw attention to the soul healing available through Christ. For Gregory, as well as other early Christian writers, Christ was both the Great Physician and the medicine of salvation. Christ was the prescription and the prescriber. In contemporary society, the church has outsourced its healing ministry to physicians and mental health counselors. An important aspect of the church's ministry today is to reassert its necessary role in the healing of the whole person.*

tude in mind. For even if our lives are lived with openness toward God, human nature remains tainted by sin. Eventually, some sin will sneak in and slowly leave its mark, making us insensitive to God's call. If this happens, God has provided us a remedy for our predicament: regret leading to repentance.

Yet it seems to me that we have only scratched the surface of the meaning Jesus the Word intends to communicate. I think if we dig deeper into the meaning of the passage we will find a deeper sense of mourning is available to us: the development of an enduring disposition of sorrow. For if the Word meant to suggest only a change associated with turning toward God, then I think it would have been more appropriate to say "those who *have* felt regret leading to repentance" rather than "those who continue to practice regret leading to repentance." Following the previous illness/healing example, we typically refer to those as blessed who are healed, and not those who require continuous treatment. The obvious implication is that if you require ongoing treatment you're still sick.

I think there are other good reasons for us not to limit our understanding of this beatitude to only the regret of repentance. Take, for example, the life of the biblical saints. Do you think because they led blameless lives they were excluded from the blessing associated with this beatitude? Or do you think John was greedy? Or Elijah an idolater? What sin—big or small—is referenced in Scripture to either of these saints? Think about it! Do you really think they didn't experience the blessedness offered by the Word because they didn't live their life without God, and therefore didn't require the appropriate medical treatment—regret leading to repentance? It seems odd that such God-centered people would be prohibited from experiencing God's blessing because they neither forgot God nor were described as experiencing regret that leads to repentance. Think of it this way: If the comforting grace of the Holy Spirit is available only to those who return to God after a life of debauchery, then wouldn't it be to our advantage to turn our back on God and indulge our most base desires? But in the Bible it says, "Blessed are those who mourn, for they will be comforted." My suggestion is that we follow the Person the prophet Habakkuk described as he who "makes my feet like the feet of a deer and enables me to tread on the heights" and explore further the meaning of this saying so that we learn the type of sorrow that attracts the comfort of the Holy Spirit.

I think the best way to proceed is, first, to define the meaning of sorrow and, second, to consider why sorrow occurs in human life. Sorrow is the soul sadness at the loss of something that is deeply satisfying. It is a disposition that is not found in those whose life is immersed in happiness. Take, for example, a person who has achieved the American dream. Everything that he has set out to do has gone according to plan. He comes from a stable and loving family. He graduated from the right college and landed a great job immediately. He is happily married to his college sweetheart and the father of two delightful children. He is a pillar of his community whose advice is widely sought. His employees admire him, and his business competitors fear him. His financial wealth allows him to enjoy all the best things that life has to offer. He enjoys a round of golf with his buddies one day and competes in a triathlon the next. By the world's standards he is a man who has it all. But suppose he suffered a change in his circumstances. Maybe he was accidentally caught up in a robbery, shot in the head and severely damaged in his cognitive abilities. Suddenly, robbed of his ability to relate to others and no longer able to manage his business, it would be fitting for him to be grieved by his loss. A person in these circumstances we would describe as sorrowful, which fits with our earlier definition of sorrow as the painful emotional disposition caused by the loss of something deeply satisfying.

Proceeding forward on the basis of this understanding of sorrow from everyday life we now can work our way toward that sorrow that is unknown. (This is the sorrow that the Bible describes as blessed.) Before we continue I want you to consider the following question: Is it is reasonable to believe that people will get upset over the loss of something that they never knew they owned? Of course not! People are not wired to get upset over something they're unaware they are missing. But what if we are missing something of infinite value? Would we live our life differently if we became aware that we lost something of significance? I think we would.

Maybe an illustration might shed some light on our subject.

Let's suppose that we find two persons living in a deep cavern completely cut off from light. The first person was born and lived her whole life in the cavern, and the second lived above ground for many years but was banished to the darkness of the cavern for some unknown reason. It makes sense that their present circumstance—the absence of light—will affect each person differently. For the second person, who knows what she is missing, the absence of light is a dreadful loss; for the first person, the absence of light is not that big of a deal because she has no comprehension of what she is missing. The second person, driven by the desire to see again, will always be searching for ways to get back what was lost. But the person born in darkness is completely comfortable growing old in the darkness, assured she is living the good life because she has never experienced anything different.

Don't you think something similar might be said about *sorrow that is blessed*? A person who truly understands what it means to live fully and completely in the presence of God, and then reflects on the poor quality of his experience of God in this life, will feel a deep sense of loss, because he knows he is far away from his deepest desire. It seems to me that if we look at it this way, then it's not that Scripture is saying that grief is blessed; rather, it is the sadness caused by the realization that our true Good and the desire of our heart is not fully available to us in this life.

Let's take this analogy to the personal level: What is the light missing from our darkened condition? Before you answer, do you think it is possible for us to know what we don't know? Can we design a scientific experiment that will allow us to investigate what we hope to uncover? I don't think so. No words or theoretical constructs are available to us that would come close to describing the reality of such a light. Even if we made up our own terminology, how could we name the undetectable or describe the non-material? How do you draw something that does not have form? Or understand what is not detected in space or time? Or get a handle on something that has no limitation? Or who is Life and brings into existence all things that are considered good? Or who is identified by the most awe-inspiring titles we can dream up? By what way of mental inquiry can this absolute good and beauty become known to us, this goodness that can be contemplated but not observed? By what means can we detect that which gives life to everything but is itself infinity and needs no generation?

So I do not lose your attention, maybe we should stop here in our effort to describe the indescribable. Even if I kept going, our efforts would fall short because our topic is beyond human comprehension. Don't think our efforts have been in vain or without purpose. The simple fact that we are unable to perceive our subject illustrates its greatness. The inadequacy of our ability to know the really Real should produce a growing sense of sadness in us as we recognize the chasm between us and the really Real is so great that we cannot know the unknown. Yet there was a time when we did have access to the really Real, even though it has always been beyond our methods of scientific inquiry. Yet there was a time when we did have access to the really Real. In fact, before the fall humanity had such access and knowledge of the really Real that they would be almost unrecognizable to us, given that humanity was fully formed to the authentic image of the Son. For all the attributes that we apply to the Son of God applied also to human beings: never-ending and blessed, independent and self-determining. Human life was lived free of pain and pointless work. Human beings lived their lives with God and knew the really Real without distortion.

The beginning chapter of Genesis tips us off to these things when it describes the first humans as being made in the image of God, living in paradise and taking pleasure in the things that grew there. They enjoyed the fruits of things like life and knowledge. Indeed, if these things were once ours, how can we not grieve over our unfortunate situation when we compare our former happiness with the tragedy of our present situation? The dignified has been cut down. The image of the heavenly has been dragged through the mud. What was created to lead now cleans toilets. What was designed for never-ending life with God has been devastated by death. Human beings, who once lived in the affluence of the garden paradise, have been evicted and relocated to a disease-ridden landfill of backbreaking work, exchanging a life free from emotional disorder and temptation for a life contaminated by suffering.

Once self-determining and independent, human beings are now controlled by so many great evils that their oppressors can hardly be counted. Each passion is in us, and as soon as we allow ourselves to be controlled by them, they become the master and we the slave. They take up a stronghold in the soul like a dictator. Our misdirected thoughts serve as the agents of our demise. Anger, fear, spinelessness, disrespect, hatred, dissension, callous cruelty, envy, flattery, viciousness and resentment—all these negative passions collude against us, enslaving our soul like it was a prisoner of war.

If one were to add to these the physical anguish caused by diseases and infections, from which human nature was originally exempt, then our tears would multiply as we pondered our present circumstances in contrast to when things were good. For this reason, it appears, the deeper meaning of Jesus' teaching that the sorrowful are to be blessed means that the soul should concern itself with the really Real and not be taken in by the deceitfulness of our present life. It is impossible for anyone who has seen these things clearly to live without grief over his or her situation, or not to be convinced that a person immersed in a hedonistic lifestyle is miserable.

I think animals provide a good example of this reality. Animals are devoid of reason, which from the perspective of human beings is something to be pitied. Yet animals seem to be completely unaware of their bad luck. On the contrary, they seem quite content in the pleasures that their lives entail. The horse struts, the bull kicks up dust, puppies roll around in the grass, and calves frolic in the field; every animal has a distinctive trait by which it conveys pleasure. Yet if they somehow became self-aware they would not continue to spend in pleasure their naïve and miserable lives. People in the mad pursuit of pleasure (think *Jersey Shore* cast members), cheerfully ignorant of the really good life in Christ, are like simplistic farm animals in their pursuit of pleasure.

It is difficult for a person captivated by their current situation to be on the lookout for something better. Yet if a person does not seek, he will not find what comes only to those who seek. This is the reason why Jesus calls mourning blessed, not for its own sake but for what comes from it. The overall context of the saying substantiates that sorrow is blessed because of the comfort received. Notice that when he says, "Blessed are those who mourn," he doesn't end the sentence there but adds, "for they will be comforted."

I'm convinced that Moses, a hero of the faith, anticipated this spiritual truth. (It was the Word who gave Moses the laws and instructions concerning the observance of the Passover celebration that anticipated the announcement of this spiritual truth . . . but I digress.) Moses instructed the Israelites to eat unleavened bread and to season their food with bitter herbs during the Passover festival. Consequently, by analogy to Israelite Passover rituals, if we hope to participate in the great heavenly banquet, in this life bitter experiences must be mixed with the joy we experience in walking with God.

Another hero of the faith, David, though reaching the pinnacle of ancient life—kingship—generously peppered his life with bitter herbs, grieving over his extended journey in this life. Seemingly about to collapse with longing for better things, he says, "Alas to me! for my dwelling in an alien land is made long" (Ps 120:5 wyc). In another psalm, intently gazing at the beauty of the divine sanctuary, he says that he faints with longing, for he perceives the lowest post in the sanctuary to be of greater value than the highest position in this world (see Ps 84).

If you want an even better illustration of what it means that the sorrowful are blessed, there is no better place to go than the story of Lazarus and the rich man. "Child, remember," said Abraham, "that in your lifetime you got the good things and Lazarus the bad things. It's not like that here. Here he's consoled and you're tormented" (Lk 16:25). It seems right that we should experience suffering in this life, seeing that we were separated from God's good plan for us by Adam and Eve's stupidity. God commanded that we should enjoy everything available to us untainted with evil; he forbade linking the experience of evil with good. Yet, through unrestrained consumerism, that is, our first parents eating from the tree of the knowledge of good and evil, we voluntarily grabbed for ourselves the opposite. Another way to state this fact—we tasted disobedience to the Word of God. And as a result, the life we live now is made up of both—sadness as well as happiness.

Life is to be lived in two realms, and as such, life is experienced according to the different characteristics of each realm. The happiness we experience is twofold: the first belonging to this life and the second to the life we look forward to in hope.

It makes sense to conclude that it is blessed to reserve our helping of happiness for what's really valuable in the life to come and take on our portion of sorrow in this fleeting and short-lived life. We shouldn't consider it a loss if we are deprived of a few pleasures in this life. Rather, the real loss would be to enjoy these temporary flings at the expense of a better reward in the future. Therefore, if it is true happiness to experience never-ending joy in eternity, then it follows that it is necessary to have the opposite experience in this life. It all makes sense then—why those who experience sorrow in this life are blessed because they will be comforted in the never-ending life to come. Now the source of this comfort is found in the Comforter. The gift of consolation is the work especially associated with the Spirit, of which we are made worthy by the grace of Jesus Christ, to whom be the glory forever and ever. Amen.

SERMON

4

Blessed are they that hunger and thirst after
justice: for they shall have their fill. (DRA)

*You're blessed when you've worked up a good appetite for God. He's
food and drink in the best meal you'll ever eat.*

There are instances where people are malnourished but not interested in food. Their body no longer functions properly, and
as a result, it sends signals to the brain that it is full and cannot
eat anymore. Their natural inclination for survival is dulled because they are duped into thinking that their bodies are properly nourished. Sometimes this can occur because of a blockage
in the intestines or abdomen. If this is the case and the blockage is removed, typically the body's desire for food will return.
The return of a healthy appetite will be viewed by the doctor as
a good sign on the road to recovery.

At this point you might be asking yourself—why is he discussing intestinal blockages and the like? As we have said in previous sermons, Jesus the Word helps us reach the next stage in our spiritual formation by guiding us as we slowly scale the ladder of the Beatitudes. The next rung in the ladder of formation for us is *Blessed are they that hunger and thirst after justice: for they shall have their fill.* It makes sense that this is the next step. By making it this far, we cleansed our spirit of much of the waste and toxins accumulated from years of poor spiritual habits. Consequently, we are now more likely to desire spiritually nutritious food, like justice.

Trainers and nutrition experts agree that to be in top physical condition and maintain muscle mass requires eating adequate amounts of healthy foods. Common sense tells us that it is not possible to consume adequate amounts of protein and calories if one doesn't eat. And it is unlikely that people will eat if they do not have an appetite.

Now, most people I know would agree that strength and stamina are one of the good things of life. Yet strength is maintained only if a person's body absorbs adequate amounts of nutrients and proteins. To break it down further we can say that in order to stay healthy we need a vigorous appetite for healthy foods. Let's be clear: we need both—"vigorous appetite" and "for healthy foods"—in order to remain in top condition. If we gorge ourselves on fries and hamburgers it will be impossible to stay fit. But if we never feel the desire to eat, like a person with anorexia, we will soon lose all our strength. Consequently it makes sense for us to affirm that an appetite is a blessing since it is the source and cause of our strength.

Not everyone likes the same food. The old saying "Variety is the spice of life" applies to our menu preferences. Some people like hot and spicy, others sweet or sour, and still others prefer their food salted. This analogy holds true for food that nourishes the soul. All of us are formed with different desires. Some people desire status, riches or fame. Others become foodies consumed with finding just the right taste to satisfy their palate. Others dine on their resentment like some toxic chow. And then there are those who have a hankering for that which is good. Good food is good food no matter when and where it is served. Food that is naturally good is not good because it is expensive or prestigious. It is good because of its natural qualities. This is why Jesus the Word does not call those who are simply famished blessed but those whose longing is for true justice.

Here's the question: What is justice? I think this is where we should start an explanation of the verse because once we understand the biblical meaning of justice, its beauty will awaken our desire for it. It has been my experience that people typically do not desire what they do not know. As a result, because they do not know what the really good life entails, their enthusiasm to do good is underdeveloped. So the question for us, as church leaders, to ask is: How do we arouse their desire to pursue the really good life if that life is unknown to them? The simple answer is to make the unknown known. How do we accomplish this task? Through storytelling. We tell stories that provide us an inspiring alternative to the mundane world where everything remains the same.

The common definition of justice derives from the philosophers. They argue that justice is the disposition to distribute what is fair and suitable according to each person's need. The technical name for this form of justice is distributive justice. As an example of distributive justice, if a person is empowered by a charitable organization to assist those afflicted by some catastrophe, she is called just if she distributes the money fairly and according to need. Likewise, a judge is not supposed to play favorites, but rather, following the facts, punish those who deserve it and exonerate those who are innocent. In civil cases, the judge should rule according to the truth. If a judge acts according to this pattern, then she is considered just. In addition, tax rates should correspond to a person's income. Anyone who exercises authority over another person or persons should exercise his responsibility objectively and not yield to his selfish desires. An authority figure who acts accordingly will be considered just. By the definition provided by the philosophers, each of the preceding examples would be considered persons who acted justly.

Yet, as I search the Scriptures and contemplate the laws of God I have come to the conclusion that God's definition of justice must go beyond mere distributive justice. Let me show you what I mean. First, we know from our reading of the Gospels that salvation offered by God through Christ is for everyone, not just for the powerful. Another way we might say this fact: The salvation of God is equally accessible to all. Second, from our experience living in the world we recognize that only a few people occupy the positions we discussed above as positive examples of distributive justice. For it is only for a few to be a king or governor, to be appointed a judge or given financial oversight or administration. The majority of people go through life with little influence on how things get done. The question must be asked: How can we accept this definition of justice as true in light of the fact that it is not equally accessible by all? For according to worldly standards, equality is the goal of the just. But the fact that economic and political power is in the hands of the few negates this definition of justice because reality shows the unfairness of life.

What then is the kind of justice that belongs to all? What then is the justice for those who put their hope in the gospel?

Whether they were born into affluence or into poverty, whether slave or master, whether a blueblood or blue collar, no circumstance increases or decreases the quality ascribed to the just. Think about it: How can you say that the poor beggar Lazarus was just if the virtue of justice can be claimed only by those with economic or political power? Didn't he beg outside the house of the rich (Lk 16:20)? Lazarus lacked access to the levers of power. He didn't give money to those in need or make judgments on behalf of the poor. Thus, according to this worldly definition, Lazarus would not be judged as just. If being just consists in ruling, administrating or distributing, then anyone with a job description that does not include these would be outside the scope of justice. How then can someone deserve to enter the heavenly rest if he hasn't performed these duties typically associated with this worldly account of justice? I hope you see my point here. We must go beyond this definition and search out a kind of justice that yields the promise to those who desire it. For Jesus says, "Blessed are they that hunger and thirst after justice: for they shall have their fill."

For most of us there are a variety of foods available to us every day, though in many instances the foods we choose are not good for us. It is the same way in the spiritual life. We have a number of spiritual foods available to us that will either provide spiritual nourishment or contribute to our unhealthiness. Therefore, it is imperative that we discern between those spiritual foods that are useful and those that are harmful to our soul. If we don't, we might bite into something that brings death rather than life. The best place to learn what foods contribute to our spiritual well-being is by studying the life of Jesus.

Jesus shared in our full humanity except for sin. He shared in all our sufferings, including the fact that at times he felt the pains of hunger. It should be made clear Jesus didn't think of hunger as a sin. He accepted a healthy appetite for food as a normal and natural bodily impulse. Following his baptism Jesus went forty days without food, and afterwards his stomach ached for food. When the architect of temptation, the devil, realized that Jesus was famished, he immediately suggested that Jesus satisfy his appetite with stones, which we know means he wanted to distort Jesus' desire for wholesome food for something twisted. He says, "Speak the word that will turn these stones into loaves of bread" (Mt 4:3).

This might not be readily apparent to most of my listeners, but it is as if the devil is saying, "Don't eat food produced by farming and growing crops." But what is wrong with farming? Why would you reject the seed and its produce? It is as though you are saying that God, our Creator, doesn't feed us properly! Are you trying to tell us that rocks are a better food source than grains? If this is so, then the wisdom of God is mistaken about what is necessary for life. The devil says, "Speak the word that will turn these stones into loaves of bread." He says the same thing, even today, to those who are beguiled by their desire for food. And in most instances he persuades those who look to him to turn stones into bread. By whose counsel, if not the devil's, does the appetite go beyond the boundary of need? He is the same one who rejects food made from grains and inflames the appetite for things unnatural.

Those who gulp down meals made from stone reveal their greediness in their ostentatious dinner parties with their exotic dishes served on expensive tableware. These parties paid for by money made unjustly are designed only to impress and go far beyond what is necessary for life. Ask yourself: What do expensive silverware and serving trays have to do with our natural need for food?

Before you answer that, let's first answer this question: What is hunger? It seems obvious that it is the desire for food that the body needs. After a long day of work, the body has spent its stored energy and needs that energy replaced by taking in the necessary nutrients. It is natural then for the body to desire something to eat like bread. But if someone munches down a handful of diamonds instead of bread, with what is the body's need for energy satisfied? You might see what I'm trying to get at here. If a person cares for material goods more than food that his body needs, then, in the language of the Gospel, he is infatuated with stones. While it would be natural for him to seek out the food that is truly satisfying, he is busy looking for something else.

Hunger pains are nature's way of saying that the body needs food because the energy expended needs to be replaced. But are you listening to nature? If you were, you would give the body what it needs. Instead you scour over Pottery Barn catalogs dreaming up the perfect dinner table. You waste your time looking for the perfect piece of granite to cover your kitchen counters and for the perfect hutch to display your exquisitely crafted china. Your body wanted bread, and instead you crafted the perfect kitchen with stainless steel appliances, copper-bottomed cookware, a wine rack and a thousand other knick-knacks that have nothing to do with what you really need. Take a hard look at how you live: Are you not listening to the one who says look at the stone? I could go on and on about this shameless materialism that grips our culture, but it would be useless to go over this self-indulgent lifestyle in more detail.

Our enemy gives us this advice on the matter of food; these are the suggestions that come from turning to stones instead of being satisfied with the everyday use of bread. Now let's make it clear that just because we overcome temptation does not mean we will eliminate our hunger, as if hunger were the cause of evil. Rather, we remove the excess, which our crafty enemy intertwines with our actual need, and allow our body to tell us what it needs. As an example: when you make wine it produces both the grape juice and a frothy layer on top. You don't throw out the wine because of the froth; rather, you use a strainer to separate the froth from the juice and thereby purify the grape juice. Jesus the Word acts in the same way. He knows what is natural to human nature and what is not. He did not eliminate hunger, because it is essential to human well-being, but he sifted out and disposed of the excess that had been mixed up with legitimate need. He accomplished this when he claims that he knows the bread, which by God's design, is good for us (see Mt 4:4). As a result, if Jesus was hungry, we may say that this hunger is blessed in us if it conforms to the hunger he experienced. Therefore, if we know what the Lord hungered for, then we would undoubtedly know the meaning of this beatitude.

So the question that seems appropriate to ask: What is the food that Jesus doesn't feel guilty to crave? After Jesus' conversation with the Samaritan woman, Jesus said, "The food that keeps me going is that I do the will of the One who sent me" (Jn 4:34). The will of the One who sent him is clear: "He wants not only us but *everyone* saved, you know, everyone to get to know the truth we've learned" (1 Tim 2:4). We know that the Father yearns for everyone to be saved, and therefore if our life is the food of Jesus, we know how to put our soul hunger to work. What is it? It is this that our soul should hunger and thirst for—our own salvation and God's will, which is that everyone should be saved. We now understand how such a hunger should come to be in us. For a person who longs for the justice of God has found what really is to be desired. But we know that our appetite is more than eating, so if a person stops at hungering for justice as food she would remain only half-filled. Justice is also a matter of drinking, in order that the intense sensation of the longing may be captured by the feeling of thirst. When we are thirsty our parched throat burns and may be satisfied only by drinking. Though our appetite for food and water is similar they do take different forms. The Word uses these differences to express our deepest longing for the Good and calls blessed those who both hunger and thirst for justice. The object of our longing is big enough to meet our hankering in both ways: solid food for the hungry and drink for the thirsty person who works hard to grab hold of grace.

*Blessed are they that hunger and thirst after justice, for they shall be satisfied.* A person who is really digging into this Scripture might ask if this blessing applies only to the virtue of justice, or does it hold true for the traditional virtues like self-control, wisdom and good sense? The answer is simple: Justice is one of the virtues, and it is a customary practice in Scripture to sort out the meaning of the whole by focusing on a part. As an example, the prophetic writer says, "I am the LORD" (Is 42:8 NIV), and speaking in the person of God says, "This has always been my name, and this is how I always will be known" (Ex 3:15). And then in another place the writer says, "I-AM-WHO-I-AM" (Ex 3:14) and in another, "I'm compassionate" (Ex 22:27). There are numerous other examples of names used for God in Scripture that adequately capture his majesty. Consequently, it is right for us to conclude that in Scripture when one name is mentioned, the whole inventory of names is to be called to mind. Let's make sure we are on the same page: Don't make the mistake and think if God is called "Lord" he isn't also the other things as well; rather, it is through this one name all the others are expressed.

Following this example, it is reasonable to conclude that in the language of the divinely inspired Scripture, we may grasp many things through only the mention of a part. Therefore, it follows, if the Word calls blessed the hunger of those who long for justice, then he means to include all the other virtues. Hence a person is equally blessed if she hungers for good sense, courage, self-control, or anything else that may be considered a virtue. The nature of virtue is such that if one virtue is practiced independently of the other virtues, it is not perfect virtue because whenever one form is practiced in the absence of other virtues, their opposite will always fill in the void. The opposite of self-control is decadence, or the opposite of good sense is stupidity, and so with every idea of good there exists its opposite. As a result, if justice didn't include the other virtues, what remained could not be called good. For it is highly unlikely that someone would say justice is idiotic or reckless, wicked or anything else identified with evil. It makes sense then if justice cannot be conceived as compatible with anything base, then of course it embraces all that is good. So every virtue is summed up under the name of justice. And those who hunger and thirst for justice are dubbed blessed by the Word, who promises to fulfill their longings.

For the Word says, *"Blessed are they that hunger and thirst after justice, for they shall have their fill."* I think the saying means something like this: None of the pleasures strived for in this life are satisfying to those who chase after them, but, as the writer of Proverbs says, like a leaky jug so is time spent in the pursuit of pleasure (see Prov 23:27). The frantic attempt to fill a leaky jug provides us a good picture of the futility of the never-ending pursuit of pleasure. This desire for pleasure is an abyss that even after repeated attempts to fill is never satisfied. Who has known the greediness of a Wall Street broker to be satisfied after he makes his first million? What celebrity seeker stops her attention-grabbing exploits once her goal is achieved? Take, for example, people who indulge their sensuality by overstimulating their senses with entertainment or gorge themselves on fine dining—what is achieved of lasting value? Doesn't the sense of satisfaction evaporate into thin air as soon as it is over?

Convinced that the promises of pleasure are false, we learn from our Lord, our teacher of the really real, that the only thing of enduring value is the single-minded pursuit of the virtuous life. For if persons truly set their mind to pursuing abstinence, self-control, fidelity to God, or any of the Gospel commands, they would experience a genuine delight that would not fade away but would endure for a lifetime. Why is this true? Because these are habits and dispositions that can be practiced throughout life's various stages. Better yet, these are things that don't grow wearisome over time. For we can always practice self-control and purity; we can be authentic in doing good and refrain from participating in evil as long as we keep our intention focused on virtue. The good news is that when we live this way the practice itself results in a profound sense of delight. But those who squander their lives chasing after foolish lusts, even if they are always engaged in decadence, will eventually not take pleasure in them. For nausea caused by overindulgence brings to a halt the cravings of the glutton, and the passion of the drunkard is extinguished at the same time as his thirst. This is the way it is when it comes to bodily indulgence. The body can take only so much before it needs a timeout in order to revive its desire. The life of virtue is the opposite. It doesn't need a timeout in order to be refreshed. It is never dulled by overindulgence. Quite the opposite, in fact: the virtuous life continually offers its practitioners a fresh experience of its delights. This is why the promise of the Word is good news because those who hunger for good things shall be filled, not in such a way that their desire is dulled but rather is invigorated.

The other take-away point from Jesus' teaching is: Don't waste your energy pursing things that will ultimately end in nothing. It is simply foolhardy to make these your life's ambition. It is like people trying to catch their shadow. They can pursue it forever, but it will always elude their grasp. A wiser course of action would be to direct your attention to objects which if pursued would be made your own. If a person desires virtue, he makes goodness his very own, for he sees in himself what he has most wanted. Think of it this way—blessed is the person who hungers after self-control, for he shall be filled with purity. Filled with the result of virtue brings about not an aversion but a deeper desire. These do not play against each other

### Never-Ending Pursuit of God

*For Gregory, perfection is progress itself: the perfect person is the one who continually grows in knowledge of God. This progress does not have a limit because our desire, the Trinity, is limitless. As a result, when we experience God in prayer, we experience the paradox of the deep satisfaction of God's presence, and yet, at the same time, we experience God's absence because he remains constantly beyond us. In the life to come we will continue to grow in our knowledge and love of God. Our knowledge of God's love will, paradoxically, grow without the awareness of less. Gregory's compelling insight was captured well in the final book of C. S. Lewis's Narnia Chronicles: "Further up and further in. . . . The further up and further in you go, the bigger everything gets. The inside is larger than the outside."*

but add to each other. Virtuous desire is followed by acquiring what is desired, and the goodness experienced internally simultaneously fosters unceasing joy in the soul. It is the amazing quality of the good life that not only do you enjoy it when practicing it, but additionally it brings happiness at every moment of time. If a person lives rightly, she enjoys her action in three ways: remembering the past, in the present action, and the expectation of the future reward. You see, virtue is both the work and the reward for those who put it into practice.

Please bear with me a little longer as I dig a little deeper into the meaning of this beatitude and propose a bold interpretation. I believe that through the ideas of virtue and justice the Lord has in mind himself as the desire of his hearers. Jesus became God's wisdom, justification, sanctification, redemption and the living water and the bread that came down from heaven. In Psalm 42, David makes known his desire for justice when he asks God: "I'm thirsty for God-alive. I wonder, 'Will I ever make it—arrive and drink in God's presence?'" It seems to me that David knew this through the inspiration of the Holy Spirit, since he also said that this desire would be fulfilled. "I will be seen in justice," he says, "I shall be satisfied when thy glory shall appear" (Ps 16:15 LXX). Now I believe that this is the Word of God himself, the true virtue, the good not tainted by evil and which embraces every model of goodness. He is, according to Habakkuk, the virtue that has sheltered the "heavens" (Hab 3:3 NIV).

It is right then to say that those who hunger for this justice of God are called blessed. In fact, a person who has tasted the Lord, similar to expression in the psalms (Ps 34:8 NIV), which may be understood to mean receiving God inwardly, has become filled with him for whom she thirsted and hungered. This happens in accordance with his promise: "We will come to them and make our home with them" (Jn 14:23 NIV). (Of course, the Holy Spirit made his home there first.) You know, as I come to think of it, I believe Paul tasted these fruits, and he experienced both fullness and the continuing desire for more. His fullness is attested to when he says that "Christ lives in me," and his enduring hunger is exemplified in his ongoing pursuit of those things before him: "Not that I've already reached the goal or have already completed the course. But I run to win" (Phil 3:12-13 GW).

Let me give one more illustration to help you understand what I'm trying to say. Suppose there was a fruit that was completely absorbed by the body such that nothing was excreted and all its nutrients and substance were used by the body to grow in stature and physique. Then the body would grow like it was on steroids, and not only would it be bigger but also it would be taller, converting its entire daily intake into physical growth. It is the same way with justice and all the other virtues associated with it, since spiritual food when consumed continually increases the spiritual capacity of those who dine on its delicacies. So now understanding what Jesus called a "blessed hunger," and expelling the glut of evil, let us hunger for the justice of God, so that we may be overfilled with it, in Christ Jesus our Lord, to whom be the glory forever and ever. Amen.

Blessed are the merciful,

for they will be shown mercy.

*You're blessed when you care. At the moment of being "care-full,"
you find yourselves cared for.*

Perhaps a good way to start today is to compare this verse with
Jacob's dream of a ladder that was set on the ground and reached
all the way to heaven. Angels of God were going up and going
down, and at the top of the ladder was God, the reward for
those who reached the top (see Gen 28:10-13). The Beatitudes
of Jesus are similar to Jacob's ladder. The Beatitudes are like
rungs on the ladder; each step up the ladder leads to higher
spiritual truths. I believe what was suggested by Jacob's ladder
was the life of virtue. God instructed Jacob this way in order
that he might learn and explain to those who came after him

that there is no other way to grow up to God than by tending to spiritual truths. Accordingly, the attitude required to complete this arduous journey is an unceasing desire for these higher spiritual truths.

Furthermore, we must not be content with our past spiritual achievements and should count it as a loss if we fail to move forward in the spiritual life. Similar to Jacob's ladder, the teachings of the Beatitudes, one above the other, train us to approach God, the really blessed and the source of all blessedness. It makes sense, then, similar to our approach to the Wise through wisdom and the Pure through purity, that we are made friends with God, the Blessed One, by way of the blessings of the Beatitudes. For blessedness is God's way of being. This is made plain by Jacob's vision of God standing at the top of the ladder. To participate in the Beatitudes then is nothing less than communion with God, to which our Lord lifts us up by his words of instruction.

It seems to me that our Lord forms into his image the person who hears his words and puts them into practice. For he says, "You're blessed when you care. At the moment of being 'carefull,' you find yourselves cared for." There are many Bible passages in which the saints of old call on the power of God by referring to God as "caring" or "merciful." David does so in the Psalms, Jonah in his prophecy (Jon 4:2), and Moses does so in many places. If the title "caring" is appropriate to God, what else is the Word trying to do than invite us to become his image, since we are to be formed in the character of God? Follow the logic; if God is called "caring" by the divinely inspired Scriptures, and Divinity is in fact blessedness, then it follows that if a person becomes caring, even though human, she is to be considered worthy of divine blessedness, since she has realized the quality attributed to God. For "the Lord is gracious and righteous; our God is full of compassion" (Ps 116:5 NIV). We call God blessed because he is caring and compassionate. Doesn't it make sense that if we share in the same name and character of God that we should be considered blessed?

Now Paul says we should "eagerly desire the greater gifts" (1 Cor 12:31 NIV). Humans by nature are predisposed toward the good, so the goal is not to convince ourselves to yearn for good things but to steer clear of making poor decisions about what is good. This is one of the biggest challenges we face in life: to clearly differentiate between what is good and what is good only in appearance. For if we saw evil without make-up, as it were, and not obscured by the appearance of good, we would not so easily be attracted to it. Therefore, we need to put on our thinking cap in order to correctly perceive the true beauty of its meaning and then conform ourselves to it. An example of this is the idea of God, which is naturally rooted in human nature. Some people, badly informed about the true God, make bone-head mistakes when it comes to the object of worship—God. Some really do worship the true God whom we know as Father, Son and Holy Spirit, but others think of God as if he were a creature and thereby open the door to all kinds of theological blunders. And so it is with the stuff we are considering here. If we don't take hold of its real meaning, the consequences for us will be steep.

What does it mean to be care-full or compassionate? And what is its function? And how is a person blessed who receives back what she gives? For Jesus says, "You're blessed when you care. At the moment of being 'care-full,' you find yourselves cared for." The most obvious meaning is that human beings are to be kind and compassionate to each other because of the fickleness and inequality of human dealings, since not everyone is born under the same circumstances whether in terms of status, physical well-being or other resources. In most cases life is divided up into the haves and the have-nots, separated according to slaves and masters, wealth or poverty, the valued or the disrespected. In order to balance the inequalities of life the person in need should benefit from the one who has a larger portion; that is, the one who is lacking should be filled from the abundance of the other. This is the prescription of mercy toward those in need. A person will not be moved to heal the pains of his neighbor unless his soul is first softened by mercy toward him. This is obvious since mercy is the opposite of cruelty. The hardhearted and cruel person is unavailable to those who seek him out, while the caring person, available to the other through sympathy, becomes to the hurting person exactly what he requires. To encapsulate the previous example in a short definition: Compassion is intentional distress that identifies with the suffering of others.

I realize for some of you I have not made the meaning clear enough, so let's try to get at it through another definition. Compassion is a loving identification with those in misery. Just as hardheartedness and malice originate in hate, so compassion flows from love, for without love compassion cannot exist. In fact, if one wanted to dig in to the distinctiveness of compassion, one would find two qualities: a growing attitude of love combined with an understanding of the emotional ache of another. It is not unusual for our friends and our enemies to be willing to share in our prosperity, but the willingness to share in our misfortune is unique to those who are governed by loving kindness. I think most people would agree that practicing a life of love is the best way to live. Compassion is the deepening of love. As such, compassionate persons are truly blessed since they have reached the high point of goodness.

The trap here is to think that compassion is limited to material acts of kindness. But this cannot be the case, since it would limit compassion to the domain of the rich. No, I think it would be better to locate such a virtue in the intention. Take, for example, the person who wants to help another in need but can-

*Jesus said, "For judgement I have come into this world, so that the blind will see and those who see will become blind" (Jn 9:39). In popular culture, judgment is viewed negatively and equated with condemnation. Yet, judgment is more than condemnation. In controversial or doubtful matters, a judgment is required when the truth is not clear. In these instances judgment refers to the uncovering of the truth. This idea is also conveyed in an alternative translation of the Greek word for truth, "unhiddenness." In judgment the truth becomes unhidden. In Jesus, truth is uncovered and life—that is, the really good life—is made known. Those who argue that the good life is found in financial security, comfort, and lavish self-indulgence obscure the good life available in Jesus and become blind. The self-deception of a life limited by self-centeredness is "uncovered" by the teaching of Jesus on the separation of the goats from the sheep in the last judgment. Jesus' stern warning of eternal punishment awakens those lulled to sleep by a life lacking in care for others. Awakened, the formerly "blind" now receive care in the caring for others, as a gift. In the care for others they "see" the care of God. Voluntarily and regularly coming alongside the least, the last and the lost is an essential component to authentic Christian formation.*

not do so because he lacks the financial resources. He should not be considered inferior, especially in regards to the disposition of the soul, to the one who shows his intentions in his good works. It should be clear, even to those young in the faith, the benefit to human society by applying the beatitude in this way.

Similarly, suppose such an attitude to those worse off than us were present in everyone; then there would no longer be excess or neediness. Life would no longer be lived in opposition as it is now. Poverty would not be a source of heartache, slavery would no longer dehumanize, and disrespect would no longer shame. Everyone would share in common all things and, as full members of society, their lives would be characterized by equality before the law, since the haves would voluntarily share with the have-nots.

If this was the way the world really worked then there would be no excuse for hostility. Jealousy would be pointless, hatred a relic of the past, the memory of hurtful actions would be forgotten. Lying, Ponzi schemes and war, which all grow out of greediness, would be unnecessary. Once this hardhearted attitude is wiped out, then the outgrowths of wickedness would be yanked out like a noxious weed. In its place would grow peace and justice. How much better would life be if we no longer needed to rely on deadbolts and security systems for our well-being but were secure in each other? Just as the cruel and hardhearted person makes adversaries out of those who have experienced his rage, so the compassionate person becomes friends with all those who share in his kindheartedness. Compassion, therefore, is the source of kindness, the promise of love and the connection between all dispositions of love. For those concerned about their security—what could be a better way to live? So it makes complete sense that Jesus calls the compassionate person blessed when such fantastic returns are implied in the name.

What we have covered so far I believe is recognized by most as practical guidance for those who want to live the good life. Yet, the use of the future tense in the passage suggests there is more here than is perceived at first glance. He says, "Blessed are the merciful, for they will be shown mercy," which implies a reward is set aside for the future for those who practice compassion.

Let's set aside the more obvious meaning, which may be discovered by any plain reading of the passage, and peer behind the veil, that is, examine the more profound meaning of the passage. "Blessed are the merciful, for they will be shown mercy." It is possible for us to learn deeper truths from this passage because God created humans in the image of God and implanted in them the longing for what is good. He did this so that no good thing should come from outside us, but that it should be within our power to will what we want by bringing forth the good stocked up in the storehouse of our heart. Applying the logic by moving from the particular instance to the more general truth, there is no other way for a person to fulfill her longing than to take hold of it herself. As Jesus instructed his audience, "The kingdom of God is within you" (Lk 17:21 NKJV). And "Everyone who asks receives, and he who seeks finds, and to him who knocks it will be opened" (Mt 7:8 NKJV). His basic point is: To receive what we desire, to find what we seek and to go where we want to go is dependent on us and our willingness to choose what is good. Consequently, the opposite is also true, that the preference for immorality isn't because the devil made you do it but immorality comes alive through our choice. Evil is a freeloader; it can't get by unless we give it life.

There are two reasons that make it clear that humans are gifted with autonomy and free will. The first is in the fact that all actions in this life, whether good or bad, depend on your choices. Second, God's future judgment takes into account the intentions of our choices and decisions. Paraphrasing the apostle Paul, "Make no mistake: In the end you get what's coming to you—Real Life for those who work on God's side, but to those who insist on getting their own way and take the path of least resistance, Fire!" (Rom 2:7-8). As an example, a good mirror reflects accurately the face that is put in front of it—cheerful for the jovial and gloomy for the miserable. It doesn't make sense to blame the mirror for the misery in the face reflected, if the original is miserable. So it follows with God's just judgment, which treats us fairly and which reflects to us according to our own decisions.

This truth is captured in the story of the sheep and the goats, where the King states, "Come, you who are blessed," and "Depart from me, you who are cursed" (Mt 25:34, 41 NIV). Is there any reason external to their person that those on the right should be addressed sweetly and those on the left so harshly? Didn't the ones on the right receive compassion through what they had done? And those on the left who were hardhearted to their neighbor, didn't they make God hardhearted to them because of their actions?

Remember the story of the rich man who passed his life in luxury and took no compassion on the poor living in his community? In the afterlife his pleadings for compassion were not heard because he cut himself off from compassion by his actions in this life. He wasn't denied the droplet of water because it would somehow diminish heaven but because the moisture of compassion does not mix with hardheartedness. As the Scriptures instruct, "How can you make a partnership out of right and wrong? . . . Is light best friends with dark?" (2 Cor 6:14). And, "What a person plants, he will harvest. The person who plants selfishness, ignoring the needs of others—ignoring God!—harvests a crop of weeds. All he'll have to show for his life is weeds! But the one who plants in response to God, letting

God's Spirit do the growth work in him, harvests a crop of real life, eternal life" (Gal 6:7-8). I interpret the seed planted as a person's choice, and the harvest as the compensation for that choice. A good harvest abounds for the person who plants in response to God. Likewise, those who choose a life of selfishness harvest a crop of weeds. I believe you harvest exactly what you plant . . . it can't be otherwise.

"Blessed are the compassionate, for they will receive compassion." What a profound statement! The fact that no restrictions are offered suggests that we should dig a little deeper into its meaning. The beatitude doesn't inform us to whom we should show compassion but only that "blessed are the compassionate." Perhaps, if we take into account the big picture, maybe Jesus is suggesting to us that compassion flows out of the sorrow that is called blessed. In the story of Lazarus and the rich man, it seems that Lazarus, who spent his life in sorrow, was recognized as blessed. Likewise, I think, Jesus is teaching the same thing here. I look at it this way: When something bad happens to people I care about, I feel bad. Take as an example a friend who is kicked out of his home by his father, or friends who barely escape a serious wreck, or friends kidnapped or enslaved or thrown into some foreign prison. If someone we cared for experienced such adversities, our natural inclination would be to feel sadness.

But, maybe we should flip the script and apply compassion to our own situation! You see, the life we experience now is contrary to our original dignity we received before the Fall. We were made for something more. We were created for paradise, but now we live like orphans—defenseless and naked— among robbers and thieves. We should take a moment and reflect on the freedom we lost and the tyrants such as the flesh, the devil and the world, which beat us down. We were meant to live forever with God, not suffer death and bodily decay. Is it advisable, having a realistic view of our situation, to be only concerned with the misfortunes of others? Shouldn't we also feel compassion for our own heart, as we consider our current situation, and what we have lost? What could be more distressing than our current imprisonment? Instead of chillin' out in paradise, we are confined to this infuriating place. Instead of being free from temptation, we are inundated with negative thoughts and enticements to evil. Instead of hanging out with the angelic host, we are condemned to live like cattle in a feed lot.

Indeed, we exchanged a life free from emotional and spiritual disturbance for harsh taskmasters like wrath and envy. We are bullied by thoughts of malice, selfish pride, sensuous indulgence and by far the worse—greed. Greed, once it takes over the heart, is never satisfied. It is like a multiple-headed monster, which through its mouths devours meal after meal yet never fills up the stomach. In fact, these meals, rather than satisfying the stomach's craving, stokes the appetite to crave more. When we take a realistic look at the disastrous consequences of our situation, does it not make sense to feel compassion for the tragedy of our situation? But we don't have compassion on ourselves because we are oblivious to our real situation. We are like the mentally ill, whose disorder renders them unconscious to their disease. If we did wake up to both our past and present situation—as Solomon says, the wise know themselves—we would continually have compassion on our souls, and this disposition of spirit would attract the compassion of God. That is why it says, "Blessed are the compassionate, for they will receive compassion."

The passage refers to "they" and not "others." Think of it this way: It is blessed to care for one's physical health . . . because people who are concerned with their physical well-being will most likely be healthy. In the same way a compassionate person is blessed because the outcome of compassion is that one receives compassion, whether along the lines above or what we discussed earlier, which, if you remember, concerns the soul's compassion for the misfortunes of others. From my point of view either is beneficial. For the attitude that people adopt to those in need in a way has the authority of divine judgment because they become their own judge, pronouncing the verdict on themselves by their treatment of those in need. I concur with many of those who came before me with the belief that all humanity will appear before Christ in judgment, in order that each person receives his recompense for his actions—whether good or bad—performed in this life.

Now I'm going out on a limb here, but I think we can say something more about the reward the compassionate will receive at that time. First, we know the gratitude those who treated compassionately in this life will extend beyond this life into eternity. As a result, I think it reasonable to ask: What is likely to happen when they recognize their friend made through compassion at his or her hour of judgment? Are they not going to honor him or her in front of the God of all creation? And what will the soul of the compassionate feel when they hear the cheers of those they helped? What greater blessing could be added to the applause of the faithful? I believe words of the Gospel teach that those who benefited from acts of kindness will be present at the King's judgment of the just and of the sinful. His words—"whatever you did for one of the least of these brothers and sisters of mine" (Mt 25:40 NIV)—point to what will occur in heaven. By referring to "these" he indicates the presence of those who benefited from acts of compassion.

Let those who prefer lifeless stuff to the future blessing of heaven tell me what gleam of gold, what shimmer of jewels, what whim of fashion matches the good that hope offers? Especially when the King over all creation, majestically seated on the throne of heaven, surrounded by countless hosts of angels, reveals himself to humanity and everyone awakes to the awe-inspiring reality of the kingdom of the heavens. On the other side of this breathtaking reality is the dread of punishment. In between these two outcomes will stand all humanity—everyone from the beginning of creation to the end of the universe. They will exist in the tension between the fear and hope of the things to come, waffling between one and the other outcome. What reliable hope will the lover of stuff have when he sees those who have lived their life with a clear conscience begin to doubt their future as they witness others dragged off into the outer darkness by their bad conscience, which serves as their executioner? But when this person is taken in front of the Judge, escorted by the shouts of admiration and the gratitude of those who benefited from his or her good works, beaming with confidence, will he or she think earthly riches compare with the happiness of that moment? Would he or she trade this for all the gold of the world? I don't think so.

Consider the case of the person who has stocked away his financial resources in enormous safes protected by steel, bolts and locks, who thinks the growth of his personal worth preferable to putting into practice the commands of the Lord. Consider the future time when he is dragged down to the fire of darkness accompanied by the reproach of those who experienced his harshness in this life, who call out to him, "Remember that in your lifetime you got the good things" (Lk 16:25). You locked away compassion with your riches. You neglected compassion for the sake of land. You did not acquire the loving kindness needed for life here. You do not have what you did not acquire; you do not find what you did not safeguard. You do not gather what you did not spread about; you do not reap where you did not plant. Your harvest matches up to your planting. You have planted bitterness, so reap its clusters of fruit. You valued mercilessness, so enjoy what you loved. You viewed others without kindness, so now you will not be looked on with compassion. You ignored the suffering of others; you will likewise be ignored. You snubbed compassion; compassion will snub you. You avoided the poor—he who became poor for you will also avoid you.

Considering all these things, where will be the gold? Where will be your impressive stuff? Where will be the security systems that were added to protect your belongings against theft? Where will be the list of your various bank accounts? What is the benefit of all this in light of weeping and gnashing of teeth? Who will lighten the darkness, douse the flame and keep at bay the undying worm?

Brothers and sisters, in the light of what has been said, let us pay attention to the voice of the Lord, who teaches us, in this brief passage, so many things about what's really important. Let us become compassionate so that through compassion we may be blessed, in Christ Jesus our Lord, to whom be the glory and power forever and ever. Amen.

SERMON

6

Blessed are the pure in heart
for they will see God.

*You're blessed when you get your inside world—your mind and heart—put right. Then you can see God in the outside world.*

As I ponder the stirring words of the Lord, it is like I am sitting on the edge of a cliff overlooking the sea. The boundless depths of the water are reminiscent of the depths of the Lord's thoughts that are beyond my ability to describe. As some of you who live along rocky coastal regions know, it is not unusual to come across a jagged peak protruding over the sea whose side has been sheared off by erosion. Now, if you were the adventurous type you might have carefully walked over to the edge and peered over. What would you feel? A little dizzy? wobbly? Or would you feel fear mixed with exhilaration? In a similar way, my spirit also was unsteady when I immersed myself in the words of our Lord, "Blessed are the pure in heart, for they will see God." God is promising to us that God will be seen by those whose heart has been made clean. Yet, isn't this the same God of whom the Gospel writer John asserted, "No one has ever seen God, not so much as a glimpse" (Jn 1:18)? Or as Paul, the highly respected scholar of the apostolic church, affirmed, "He's never been seen by human eyes—human eyes can't take him in!" (1 Tim 6:15).

When these verses are compared with our verse, "blessed are the pure in heart, for they will see God," they appear contradictory. Yet it is a basic Christian belief that all Scripture is Spirit-inspired and useful for teaching. As a result, the bits of information and insight that the Bible provides should fit together in such a manner that they are not contradictory. If it at first glance scriptural affirmations appear contradictory, it is essential that we dig deeper and look below the surface.

Further, I am reminded of Moses' teaching on the subject: "No one can see me and live" (Ex 33:20). Moses climbed to the top of Mount Sinai only to learn that it was not possible for him to catch a glimpse of the face of God. So it is with our own reasoning; over time we keep adding facts on top of facts hoping that we may perceive the reality of God, only to find that all our intellectual efforts fall short of our desire.

In another instance we are taught that to see God is eternal life. Yet three of the most trustworthy guides in the Christian life, John, Paul and Moses, tell us that this is impossible. Do you see why I feel woozy as I attempt to comprehend the depths of these words? Our predicament may be stated this way: If God is life, then the person who does not see God does not see life. Yet, the prophets and apostles, who we confess are divinely inspired, all agree that God cannot be seen. Should we then lose hope in the possibility of experiencing Life itself? Not necessarily, because we can trust in the Lord, who supports the weak in faith. It is helpful to recall the Gospel episode in which Peter walked on the water toward Jesus only to become fearful and begin to sink. Jesus reached out and brought him to safety by lifting him up onto the solid surface of the water (see Mt 14:28-31). Likewise, if the hand of the Son of God reaches out to us and lifts us up, we will be able to stand on the solid surface of our muddled thinking. Once in the grasp of the Lord, freed from fear, we receive the gentle guidance of the firm hand of the Word. For the Lord says to us, "Blessed are the pure in heart, for they will see God."

The promise made by Jesus concerning those who should be considered blessed is staggering. In the language of Scripture, seeing means the same as to have or enjoy. In Psalm 128:5, the psalmist writes, "May you see the prosperity of Jerusalem" (NIV); this means the same as "enjoy the good life in Jerusalem." Or as the prophet writes, "Let the wicked be taken away so that he shall not see the glory of God" (see Is 26:10 LXX). In this instance "not see" means "not share in." As a result, whoever has seen God will enjoy the one thing that is all things to us. Let me explain: Scripturally speaking, when it says "we will see the glory of God," it is shorthand for the following: "We will enjoy all the good gifts of God such as eternal life, freedom from the decay of death and the never-ending happiness of the kingdom of God." In addition, we will hear the gentle voice of the Spirit in our hearts and experience constant joy and spiritual clarity. In short, we will experience all the good we long for in the goodness of God.

Yet, how does this knowledge benefit us? For the problem persists: What benefit is it to know how to see God if we do not have the capability to realize this promise?

It would be like someone saying, "It is a great thing to be in heaven because in heaven we enjoy things that cannot be seen in this life." Now if included in this statement was a description of the means of transportation that made it possible to travel to heaven, then this would be delightful news. But as long as this journey remains impossible, what is the use of being told such things? In fact, it would be cruel to describe heaven in such lofty terms and then in the next breath say there is no way for us to make this journey.

Do you think that the Lord would command something beyond our nature and boundaries of human capability? I don't think so. He would never ask us to fly like the birds without providing us wings and feathers or to live under water when he has designed us to live on dry ground. In all other examples, the law matches the capabilities of those to whom it applies and asks nothing beyond one's natural capacities. Therefore, we should be comforted that what is asked in the beatitude is not hopeless. Heroes of the faith—Paul, John, Moses and others like them—did not miss the mark in attaining the blessedness that comes from seeing God. No, for one said, "There is in store for me the crown of righteousness, which the Lord, the righteous Judge, will award to me on that day" (2 Tim 4:8 NIV), and the other leaned on the chest of Jesus, and Moses heard God's voice say, "I know you by name" (Ex 33:17). Now if these men, who tell us that to see God is beyond us, are blessed and this is achieved through purity of heart, then it follows that purity of heart—the way we become blessed—cannot be impossible. How is it then that those like Paul, speaking scriptural truth, say that seeing God is beyond us and at the same time the Lord's promise that God may be seen by the pure in heart not contradict each other?

Before we move forward, I think it would be best to address

some issues of methodology by which we might dig deeper into the subject at hand. The divine nature, whatever it might be in and of itself, is beyond human comprehension. God is unapproachable and inaccessible to human speculation. No method has been devised as a means of understanding the things way over our heads. This is why Paul describes God's ways as "beyond tracing out" (Rom 11:33 NIV), which means the way to knowledge of the divine essence is inaccessible to human rationality. The fact is, no one before us has left a trace of understanding of that which is way over our heads. God's nature is above every nature, and as such, the Invisible and Incomprehensible must be seen and known by some other way. There are many means for understanding. It is possible to see God, who has made all things in wisdom (see Ps 104:24), secondarily through the wisdom displayed in the universe. Archeologists and historians do this when they examine an ancient art work. They make rational inferences about the artist based on the work of art itself. This example is not completely accurate because what is seen is not the nature of the artist but only the artistic skill mirrored in the work.

Similarly, when we study the mechanisms of creation, we form a rational image not of God's essence but of the wisdom of him who made all things wisely. Another means for understanding is to consider why God created us. He did not create us because he had to; rather, he freely created us out of his goodness. We can say, if we think of God in this way, that we understand God according to his goodness, though again, not his essence. In fact, anything you consider that directs your attention to God's goodness is a means for knowing God, since each of these make God seen. Power, integrity, faithfulness, freedom and all such things stamp on our souls the image of a heavenly and awe-inspiring vision. What I have tried to do here is to demonstrate that the Lord speaks truthfully when he promises that God will be seen by the pure in heart. At the same time, Paul does not lie when he affirms that no one has seen God nor can see God. For God is by nature invisible. He becomes visible in his operations because he may be seen in certain aspects he possesses.

The meaning of this beatitude is not limited to the analogy drawn from operations to Operator. If this were so, then even the secular intellectuals would gain knowledge of divine wisdom and power from their study of the intricacies of the universe. Rather, I think the splendor of the beatitude, available to those who accept its counsel, is something else. I'll give a few examples to illustrate what I'm trying to say. A healthy body is considered a good thing in our society, yet happiness is found not in just knowing the principles of healthy living but in living a healthy life. Take, for example, the person who goes on and on about eating healthy, but his kitchen is filled with junk food. And because of his poor eating habits he suffers a vitamin deficiency that then leads to poor health. What good is it to such a person to talk up healthy living when in fact he is suffering poor health because of his choices?

In the same way we should understand the passage under discussion. The Lord does not say it is blessed to know something about God; rather, it is blessed to have God living in your heart. "Blessed are the pure in heart, for they will see the Lord." I'm not convinced that God promises an immediate vision of God to a person whose spiritual eyesight is purified; rather, I think we should understand this passage along the lines of what Jesus said to others: "The kingdom of God is within you" (Lk 17:21). By this I think he means that if a person's heart is purged of any disruptive affections, she will see the image of God in the beauty of her inner being. It seems to me, in this pithy statement, Jesus counsels this: In every person there is a longing to experience the really Real, and when you hear that the divine majesty is way, way above your head, that its glory is incomprehensible, its beauty is beyond words, do not give up hope in seeing what you long to behold. Why? Because it is in your reach! Inside you are the means to see the really Real. God, in the beginning, gifted you with this amazing aptitude. God impressed on your being the splendor of his likeness as though he was fashioning a replica in soft wax. The bad news is that sin obscured, like layers of accumulated grime, the divine image and made its benefits useless to you. The good news is that by practicing a life of faithfulness, you can scrub off the accumulated filth, and the beauty of the really Real will again radiate from your heart.

A good example of this is a rusty tool. With a little elbow grease and steel wool you can remove the rust and restore it to its original shiny condition. And so it is with the inner person, which the Lord calls the heart; when the rust of moral decay is scrubbed off, the heart will recover the likeness of its prototype (Jesus) and be good—for what is like the good is also good. Therefore, if a person who is pure in heart sees within himself what he desires, he becomes blessed because when he gazes on his own purity he sees the reflection of the divine image.

As an example, most people don't stare directly into the sun but observe the sun indirectly through a mirror. The reflection in the mirror is not the sun, though you can see the sun's disc shape just like those who gaze directly at the sun. So the Lord says it is with you. Even though we are too weak to look directly on the divine light, we can see the light indirectly in ourselves if we return to the grace of the image that was formed in us at the beginning of creation. For God is purity, freedom from corrupted desires and separation from all wickedness. It follows that if these good things can be found in you, then indeed God is in you. Therefore, if your mind is not watered down with any evil, free from corrupted desires and steers clear from any stain, then you are blessed because of your laserlike vision. For by becoming pure you now can see clearly what is undetectable to those not purified. With the cataract of materialism that blurred the eye of your heart removed, you now see in the radiance of your heart the blessed vision. And what is this vision? It is purity, sanctification, simplicity, and other reflections of the really Real by which God is seen.

Now I fully affirm that what has been said so far is true, but it seems that we still face the same predicament as presented at the beginning of the sermon. We know that if someone sees and enjoys heaven's amazing sights but because the way to these amazing wonders is not possible, we are left knowing that none of these amazing insights are of any value to us. So it is with the happiness that comes from a purified heart. I don't think anyone doubts that a

> **Mirror**
>
> *Gregory regards human nature as a mirror, such that the soul cannot help but assume the features of what it is turned towards. The soul mirrors what it chooses to direct its attention towards.*
>
> *Another way to say it is, what the soul contemplates is what the soul becomes. For all of us, our soul reflects what we give our attention. What does your soul reflect? If your thoughts linger on anger, if they nurture resentment or envy, or any of the other vices, your soul will distort the image of Christ to a world in desperate need to see Christ.*

person is blessed if his heart is purified, but for most of us purifying our hearts is equally as mystifying as trying to make our way to heaven. What means of transport is available for that type of trip? Where does one find Jacob's ladder or the fiery chariot that carried Elijah to heaven? Anyone wise in the ways of the heart knows that escaping from the snares of misdirected desire is impossible, or at the least impractical. Our whole life is somehow connected to passions. Our conception is the effect of the consummation of our parents' sexual desires. Our growth into adulthood and later decline into old age is fueled by desire. Misdirected desires have overwhelmed holy desires since Adam and Eve's disobedience allowed them to take root in our heart. Humans are very similar to animals in this aspect of generation. For animals in each generation inherit the traits of their parents and their parents' parents and so on. So it is with us, we inherit the sinful ways of our parents—sinner from sinner from sinner. As a result, sin—in some sense—latches onto us when we are born and grows with us until our life comes to its end.

By contrast, virtue is difficult to acquire. Even if we make it our life's pursuit, any movement we make is hardly noticeable. The Bible teaches us this fact. We all know that the path to the kingdom is difficult and goes through a narrow opening, but wide and easy is the way (like cruising downhill on a highway) that leads to wickedness and death. At the same time, the Bible, through the lives and achievements of the saints, affirms that the higher life is not beyond our reach. Again, we come back to—the promise of seeing God takes form in two ways. First, understanding the divine nature which surpasses the universe, and second, that which comes from being united with God through purity of life. The former knowledge is clearly not attainable, which is confirmed by the saints, while the latter is promised to us in the Lord's teaching, "Blessed are the pure in heart, for they will see God."

How to become pure in heart is taught throughout the Gospels. You need only to study the principles one by one to discover what it is that makes the heart pure. Wickedness can be separated into two categories: one consisting in works and the other consisting in thoughts. Wrongdoing observable in actions was punished under the law of the Old Testament. Now the Lord extends the law to cover the latter, not so much punishing the evil act but guarding against the evil taking hold in the first place. To liberate the will from evil is much better than making a person's life free from wrongdoing. Since evil can take shape in many ways, the Lord applies his own teachings to come up with the appropriate cure for each forbidden exploit.

Since anger can touch all aspects of life, he begins with a cure for it by first stipulating no anger. "You've learned," he says, "from the old law not to murder; now learn how to keep your soul from anger at your neighbor." He did not completely outlaw anger. He knew that in some instances that anger could be used toward a good end. What he does outlaw is to be angry with your brother for no good reason. This is made clear when he says, "But I say to you that whoever is angry with his brother without a cause" (Mt 5:22 NKJV). The ending clause "without a cause" shows that sometimes anger is timely, particularly when anger is directed toward the rebuke of sinful behavior. This type of anger is confirmed in the word of Scripture in the case of Phineas, when he appeased God's wrath by slaying the transgressors of the law (see Num 25:6-11).

Jesus' next move is to apply the cure to sins committed through pleasure. And by his commandment he frees the heart from the lust for adultery. Similarly, you find the Lord corrects the fault of each, one by one, by setting up in opposition his law to each vice. He prevents physical attacks from flaring up by not even permitting self-defense. He drives out the passion of greed by instructing a robbery victim to go the distance and give up what he has left to his mugger. He repairs cowardice by commanding us to hold death in contempt. Overall, you see that the Lord, by his commandments, gets to the root issues of evil. Like a plough digging into the depths of our heart, his commandments cut off the growth of weeds.

The Lord does us well in two ways: first by promising good things, and second by providing instruction that leads to the goal. If you are the type of person who thinks pursuing the good is annoying, then compare it with the opposite way of life, and you will discover how much more distressing it is, especially if you value the life to come over the present. People who hear references to hell no longer resist sin by effort and hard work, but fear awakened in the mind becomes enough to chastise one's passions. Something that is implicit in our teaching might also arouse in us a more intense desire. If the pure in heart are blessed, then it follows that the opposite is true: those with a corrupted mind are miserable because they stare into the face of our Adversary. Additionally, if the divine image is stamped on the life of virtue, then it is clear that the life of vice takes on the shape and image of the Adversary. Now certain names are used for God to account for different attributes that correspond to the good—light, life, incorruption and similar things. Conversely, everything opposite of the good is attributed to the ringleader of evil—darkness, death, corruption. Knowing the difference between a good life and an evil life suggests that we have the capability by way of our free will to choose either life path. So let us run away from the form of the devil, discarding the mask of evil and putting on again the image of God. Let us become pure in heart, in order that we might become blessed when the image of God is reformed in us through wholesome conduct, in Christ Jesus, our Lord, to whom be glory forever and ever. Amen.

S E R M O N

7

Blessed are the peacemakers,
for they will be called sons of God.

*You're blessed when you can show people how to cooperate instead
of compete or fight. That's when you discover who you really are,
and your place in God's family.*

Moses, the giver of the Law, constructed the tabernacle according to the pattern shown to him by God on Mount Sinai. At the center of the tabernacle was the holy of holies. The holy of holies was special. It was no ordinary space. It was not constructed for everyday use. This inner sanctuary was more pure and more sacred than the sacred area around it. I mention the layout of the tabernacle because I think this serves as a useful analogy to the relationship between the previous beatitudes and this beatitude. Like the outer sanctuary, the previous beatitudes taught to us by our Lord are all perfectly holy. But in this beatitude we are invited to consider what is truly the holy of holies: a refuge inaccessible to all but the very devout. The promise of our last beatitude—seeing God—is unimaginably good, but the promise of this beatitude to become children of God is, frankly, breathtaking! Words fail here. How could we possibly describe a gift of such a great promise? Whatever you can imagine about this promise, the reality of the promise is much better. Words like "good," "magnificent" and "awe-inspiring" do not do justice to the staggering greatness of this promise. This promise fulfilled is the reward that surpasses prayer, the gift that outdoes hope and the grace that exceeds our nature. What is human nature compared with the nature of God? Well, if we look through Scripture we can find all sorts of references to the low rank of human nature. Abraham describes human nature as dust and ashes (Gen 18:27). According to Isaiah, human nature is grass. David does that one better and describes human nature "as" grass. For the former says, "All flesh is grass," and the latter says, "Man is as grass." Ecclesiastes calls human nature vanity.

So this is what Scripture says about humanity, but what about God? How do you describe that which cannot be seen or heard or grasped by the heart? What words may be used to describe the really Real? What new words would I need to coin in order to describe the indescribable? Scripture makes many remarkable statements about God, but really, how do they compare with the actuality of God? Scripture teaches us as much as we are capable of understanding, but it does not disclose all that is to be known. I know this is not easy to understand, so let me give you an illustration that might help. All of us breathe in air. Some of us with larger lung capacity breathe in more air than others with less capacity. But no matter how much air we inhale, we do not breathe in all the air around us. The part we inhale is always significantly less than the whole that is still there.

So it is with what is said about God in the Bible, which was composed by writers inspired by the Holy Spirit. If we compare their understanding with ours—theirs goes beyond our understanding, yet their understanding does not reach the brilliance of the whole truth. "Who has scooped up the ocean in his two hands, or measured the sky between his thumb and little finger?" (Is 40:12). Isaiah's description of the overwhelming power of God is magnificent, but it still doesn't even scratch the surface of God's full reality. The truth of the matter is that God is beyond representation. In fact, the Bible cautions us on attempting to say too much about God. Isaiah, in the person of God, says, "So—who is like me? Who holds a candle to me?" (Is 40:25). And in Ecclesiastes it says, "Do not be quick with your mouth, do not be hasty in your heart to utter anything before God. God is in heaven and you are on earth, so let your words be few" (Eccles 5:2 NIV). In both these passages the point is: God is far above any human thought. Yet, it is to this magnificent reality that can neither be seen nor heard nor grasped that humanity, described in the Bible as grass, ashes and vanity, becomes like and receives through adoption the status of a child of God.

I'm stumped on how we are to thank God for such an extraordinary gift! I want to praise God for this extraordinary gift of grace, but my words and thoughts fall far short. What is this gift? Human beings surpass their nature; mortals become immortal; those worn out by time become renewed; the momentary becomes enduring; in short, a human being becomes a god. For if we are made worthy of becoming children of God, then it follows that we will acquire the dignity of the Father and inherit all the benefits of being a part of the family. The over-the-top generosity of our fabulously rich God blows me away. Out of his bigheartedness the Lord gives lavishly from his indescribable resources. Because he loves us so deeply, though we are disfigured by wrongdoing, he elevates us to near equal status. What else are we to make of the fact that he takes what he owns and gives it to us? Does he not by his actions promise a certain correspondence of esteem due to the relationship?

Great is the reward for completing the challenge. What is the challenge? If you make peace, he says, you will be rewarded with adoption as a child of God. I'm of the opinion that the work for which is promised such a great reward is itself an additional gift. For what can be more important than a life lived in peace? Think of a list of things that are essential to a happy life—don't they all require a life of peace to be enjoyed to their full potential? As an example, think of a person who has everything—financial prosperity, good health, spouse, children, nice home, loving parents, good employees and close friendships—all the things that make up the "good life." To make this life even more attractive, add steak and lobster dinners available to you at any time, your own private workout facility for you and your friends. Not enough? Add on-demand private movie theater, box seats at the best rock concerts and all the latest video game systems—anything that makes life enjoyable in the lives of the rich and famous. If everything I mentioned is available to you, yet peace is absent and you are caught in the middle of a war—what good are they to you? Do you see the value of peace? Peace in itself is good, but it also enhances everything else that is considered valuable in this life. Moreover, if we should suffer some hardship—which happens to all of us—in a time of peace, then the bitterness of this hardship is sweetened by the benefit of serenity and makes our suffering palatable. However, overwhelmed with the severity of war, it is likely that we will become numb to the source of our sadness. As a rule, I think private suffering is not as brutal as the suffering caused by public devastation.

To grasp this point a little better, consider what happens when you experience physical pain from two different sources. Suppose you have an inflamed tendon in your leg that produces a low level of discomfort during the day. On top of that you develop a migraine, which is so intense that you are left incapacitated. If your doctor asks, "Where does it hurt?" you most likely would forget to mention the pain caused by the inflamed tendon because the pain of the migraine would conceal the pain of the leg. This is even truer in warfare. People caught up in military struggles many times overlook other sources of discomfort. Yet, if you have become numb to painful experiences, how can you think that you would be able to enjoy pleasant experiences? The fact is: War is brutal. Surrounded by violence, engulfed in chaos, devastation becomes the norm. Soldiers fight it out in the streets causing neighborhoods to be engulfed in fear. Bloody skirmishes erupt leaving no choice but to either kill or be killed. Lying in the street are the dead, earth damp with blood and the wounded abandoned for death. It is a grim picture.

Do you think people caught up in such horrific events can ever relax and enjoy the memories of more pleasant circumstances? And even if in a quiet moment memories of more pleasant times seep into their consciousness, soon they will be swamped with thoughts of loved ones in danger. So remember when God provides by protecting you from the ravages of war—he is giving you a double gift. For one gift is the reward for completing the challenge; the other gift is the challenge itself. So, then, the wise person values peace for its own benefit even if no other reward is promised.

The discussion above provides us a glimpse into God's love for us, in that he gives us this prized reward not because of our effort but, in a sense, for our enjoyment. Peace is a basic building block for giving and receiving happiness. And our God desires for us to acquire such a quantity of peace that not only do we have enough for ourselves but also that we are able, from our abundance, to freely give it to those who do not. I remind you what he says: Blessed are the peacemakers.

A peacemaker is someone who gives peace to another. We know a person cannot give to another what he or she does not already possess. For this reason, the Lord wants you first to be filled with the benefits of peace and then pass it on to those who are in need of it. Here we do not need to be too concerned about searching for a deeper meaning for the passage, for a literal reading provides more than enough for us to obtain its benefit.

### Peace

*In our individualism sometimes we value inner peace over shared or public peace. Gregory, like the apostle Paul before him, highlights the desirability of societal peace established by civil authorities as a provision for the peace given by Jesus. The peace of Christ expresses a way of right relations with God, one's self and others. Our spirituality (right relation with God and our inner life) and justice (right relation with others) are intimately bound together. It is important for our spiritual growth to integrate our inner life with just living, for our Lord requires us "to act justly and to love mercy and walk humbly with [our] God" (Mic 6:8 NIV).*

The saying "Blessed are the peacemakers" heals many of the illnesses of the soul and in a succinct way captures the many details encapsulated in this comprehensive term.

First, let us consider what peace is. It should be obvious that peace is a loving kindness toward one's neighbor. And what then is the opposite of love? It is hatred, anger, rage, envy, nursed resentment, hypocrisy and the tragedy of war. How amazing that one word is the cure for so many kinds of soul diseases! Peace is opposed equally to the list of things just mentioned and obliterates these evils by its presence. Just like the case of disease disappearing at the onset of health, or darkness withdrawing when light shines forth, so it is when peace appears and all the unhappiness produced by its opposite fades away.

I won't go into more detail on the great benefit of peace. You are capable of thinking through what life is like for those who treat each other with jealousy and hatred. Their conversations are disagreeable. They speak past each other. Their opposite is so despised they cannot even look on the other. They take on the opposite opinion of their adversary in every instance. If one says he likes this or that, the other jumps on the bandwagon for its opposite. Therefore, our Lord wants the grace of peace to permeate our whole being like a sweet fragrance filling a room so that our lives may heal the soul sickness of others.

The unsurpassed goodness of peace might be more easily recognized if we take a moment and discuss the misery produced by attitudes and dispositions hostile to peace. It is difficult to come up with an example that illustrates the negative effects of rage, though I will try. A flawed but adequate example for our purposes is to compare the affect of a person with a severe mental illness and a person consumed with rage. The mentally ill person's eyes are bloodshot and unfocused; his speech is harsh and jumbled. It is the same for the person consumed with rage. In addition, the ill person's body shakes uncontrollably, the hands constantly move, and the head tosses back and forth. Again the description applies to both. The only difference—one acts so voluntarily and the other does so against his will. How distressing it must be to find yourself in this situation because of your poor choices!

In addition, if you encounter someone suffering this disease against his or her will, your natural inclination is to feel compassion. But if a person comes into contact with the fury of another's rage, the tendency is to mirror that rage as if it cannot be outdone. If the demon afflicts the body of the mentally ill, evil's end effect is the madman's arms flailing about wildly, whereas the demon of rage inspires movements of the body that are intended to inflict harm. For when this passion takes hold of a person it is like the saying "their blood boils over." It affects their whole body—their bloodshot eyes protrude from their sockets glaring at the victim of their rage. Their breathing becomes labored, veins in their neck pop out and their voice becomes shrill. Because they are no longer able to control their facial muscles, drool dribbles out the corners of their mouth and spit flies with every raging word. Unlike the mentally ill persons, who cannot control their arms and legs, the wrathful persons, in a fight, direct their blows to cause the most physical damage. They are even willing, like a wild animal, to use their teeth, if given the chance.

It would be extremely difficult to list all the evils that originate in rage. So it follows that the person who prevents such appalling conduct ought to be considered blessed and held in high esteem for his or her valuable action. If a doctor is honored for finding a cure for a harmful disease, how much more should a person who frees the soul from disease be revered. As the soul is superior to the body, so the soul healer is to the doctor.

But don't think for a minute I consider the disease of rage to be the most serious evil brought about by hatred. Envy and hypocrisy, in my opinion, are much worse. In this instance I would apply this principle—hidden evil is more dangerous than the obvious. Consider the case of two dogs—the one barks incessantly as you pass by the yard but does not become aggressive, while another makes no noise and attacks when your back is turned. It is the same way with envy and hypocrisy. Nursed in the depth of the heart by those full of hatred, they deceptively appear as a friend. Like smoldering embers, for a short time no flame shoots up; only a bitter smoke seeps out. Over time, because it is bottled up on the inside, soon the pressure builds, and it takes only a spark for it to explode into a flame. Likewise envy consumes the heart smoldering in secret. The disease might remain out of sight because of shame, but sooner or later it will seep out into the open. The bitterness that grows out of envy makes itself known in smirks and suppressed glee when it witnesses the trials and sorrows of the person envied.

The hidden sickness of envy etches itself into the face of its fans. The physical symptoms of a person concealing envy mirror that of a person on a deathbed—sunken eyes covered with shriveled lids, knitted eyebrows and bones protruding through stretched skin (think of Gollum in J. R. R. Tolkien's *The Lord of the Rings Trilogy*). And what is the source of this dreaded disease? The prosperity of a relative or friend or neighbor! It is crazy to think that the basis of their complaint is simply that the person who they wish would suffer misfortune does not. Their bitterness stems not from some harmful action by another but simply because the other person enjoys their life. If I could speak to that person directly I would ask him—What's wrong with you? Why are you so bitter over the success of your neighbor? What is it to you that he has a good job, accumulated a nice nest egg or his opinions are valued? Why are you upset by the success of his children or that he is happily married? Why do these things pierce your heart with grief? Look at you—your hands are always clenched and your mind is in turmoil. You do not enjoy the many wonderful things at your disposal; your food is tasteless, and over your home hangs a dark cloud of unhappiness. You are always ready to hear the worst about a person who has done well in life but ill-equipped to hear a favorable report.

If this is your disposition—why do you try to dress it up with hypocrisy? Why disguise your feelings by putting on a big show of friendship and support? Why do you greet people warmly, wishing them the best while in your heart desire the opposite? Cain, whom you resemble, was furious at the praise Abel received. Envy prodded him toward murder, but hypocrisy carried through envy's desire. For Cain, under the pretense of friendship, lured Abel into the field far from his parents' reach, and here his envy was brought into the open by murder. It should be obvious that a person who removes a disease like this from another's life, bringing together family members and friends into good relations, performs a divinely inspired work. He kicks out evil and replaces it with a share in the good. And this is the reason Jesus called the peacemaker a child of God, because he models his life on the true Son who made these things available to human beings.

Therefore blessed are the peacemakers, for they will be called children of God. Who are they? They are those who model God's love for people and in their lives make plain the nature of God's loving activity. The Lord, the giver of all good things, eradicates everything that is alien to the good. In fact, this is the work he asks you to do: expel hatred, resolve conflict, do away with envy, put a stop to fighting, root out hypocrisy and extinguish the inner resentment stemming from injuries still smoldering in the heart. And then fill the emotional space opened by their removal with their opposites. Just as light follows the departure of darkness, so also replace these destructive things with the fruit of the Spirit: love, joy, peace, goodness, magnanimity and all the other things mentioned by Paul.

How then can the dispenser of the good gifts of God not be blessed, since she imitates the gifts of God and models her own good works on God's generosity? Yet perhaps the beatitude is not only concerned with the good of others. I would argue that the best kind of peacemaker is the person who brings resolution in herself the conflict between flesh and spirit, the battle royale in her nature, so that the impulses of the body no longer go against the good guidance of the mind but become subject to a higher authority. This way a person becomes a steward of God's commandments. Now don't think that God is saying that we are governed by two different principles. Rather, understand that once the dividing wall of vice is knocked down inside us, the two—flesh and spirit—will grow together becoming one because they are both reintegrated with the good. Now, when the faithful think of God, they know that God is not divided but one without duplicity, so by such work of integration—peacemaking—humanity is freed from duality and returns where it always belonged—with the Good. And by doing so becomes one and free from deceit. Such people are completely one; their demeanor in public is the same as when they think no one is watching. It is then that the beatitude becomes true. For people who live this way are really children of God, since they are blessed according to the promise of our Lord Jesus Christ, to whom be the glory, forever and ever. Amen.

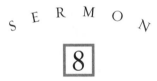

S E R M O N

8

Blessed are those who are
persecuted because of righteousness,
for theirs is the kingdom of heaven.

*You're blessed when your commitment to God provokes persecution. The persecution drives you even deeper into God's kingdom.*

We've made our way along the path of the Beatitudes and now begin the eighth leg in our journey. As with most of my contemporaries I believe that nothing is included in the Bible that does not have spiritual significance. Take, for instance, the fact that this is the eighth beatitude. Some people might want to skip over this fact and proceed directly into interpreting the text. Not me. I think its eighth position has interpretive importance. In fact, I think that if we take some time and exam-

ine the various biblical verses that reference the number eight
we will gain spiritual insight into today's verse. Two sets of
references I believe are particularly important to our discussion today. First, in our Greek version of the Old Testament
the title to Psalm 6 is "To the eighth." Second, according to the
Old Testament law, purification rites and circumcision, very
important matters in the Hebrew religion, are to take place on
the eighth day. In both cases, the reference to the number eight
is spiritually significant. And I don't think it is a coincidence
that our eighth beatitude comes at a high point of our spiritual
journey with the Beatitudes. In Psalm 6, "to the eighth" refers
to the eighth day or the age to come, which begins with the
final resurrection. On this day, time ceases and the resurrection we long for transforms our nature into something new.
Reading the Old Testament law spiritually, Hebrew purification rites point to humanity's future restoration from corruption to purity and circumcision to the stripping of the "dead"
skin—mortality, desires—humans received after the trans-
gression in the garden. And finally, the eighth beatitude refers
to the restoration of the enslaved who now are being called
back to the kingdom. In all these cases, the "eight" suggests to
us to not focus on our present circumstances but redirect our
attention toward our promised future to live fully transformed
in God's kingdom.

He says, "Blessed are those who are persecuted" for my sake,
"for theirs is the kingdom of heaven" (NIV). Listen closely to
what is being said, and understand that the purpose of your
godly struggles, the reward for all your work, the return on
your persistent efforts is to be considered worthy of the kingdom of the heavens. As a result, we no longer need to be distracted by the insignificant, seeking to secure our hope in the
unreliable and changeable. Our earthly existence is unstable

and unpredictable, but consider the movement of the stars; absent are these variations because they follow a well-thought-out progression. Do you get the importance of what the Lord is offering? The significance of the honor lies in the fact that it is not dependent on transitory circumstances, which would undermine our hope. Rather, by linking the promise to the kingdom of the heavens, he indicates the gift is totally reliable.

I believe that if the Bible is to be considered a reliable guide to the spiritual life it must be consistent. As a result, when there appears to be an inconsistency in the teaching of the Bible in its various books, it must be rigorously investigated to see if this apparent contradiction is real or not. The first inconsistency that comes to mind is that in the Beatitudes, both those who are poor in spirit and those persecuted for his sake receive the same reward, which doesn't add up because we should expect to receive the same reward only if we are engaged in the same contest. Second, why in the parable of the sheep and goats (Mt 25:31-46), when the Son of Man gathers all the nations to the kingdom of the heavens and separates those on the right from those on the left, does he do so on the basis of something different from what he states in this eighth beatitude? In the parable he suggests that the basis for this distinction is compassion, sharing of resources and reciprocated love. Yet I can't find anywhere in the parable where he mentions spiritual poverty or suffering for his sake! So what does spiritual poverty have to do with persecution? Or for that matter, what is the connection between either of these and acts of kindness? Someone feeds the hungry, or gives clothes to the shivering, or provides a room to the homeless, or visits the sick in the hospital or the convict in prison—what do these have to do with being poor or persecuted according to how we talk about these things? The former helps those less fortunate, while both the poor and the persecuted

### Martyrs

*We now define the word* martyr *as a person who willingly suffers death rather than renounce his or her faith. Originally the Greek word* mártyros *meant "to witness." Eventually, in the Christian church, "martyr" referred to those Christians who publicly witnessed to the lordship of Christ through their death. Gregory's family were faithful witnesses to the lordship of Christ in times of persecution, even to the point of death. Gregory's great-grandfather died as a martyr. Saint Macrina the elder (the patron saint of widows) and her husband, Gregory's father's parents, both suffered for their faith not only once but twice. In the first instance they were exiled. In the second and last persecution in the eastern Roman Empire, which was a particularly brutal persecution, their property was confiscated by the emperor. Jobless and impoverished, they survived only by trusting in God's care. After the last persecution they were esteemed in the church as "confessors of the faith," a very important honor in the early church. Gregory's family experienced firsthand the pain of persecution for the sake of righteousness. I imagine Gregory and his brothers and sisters grew up hearing these stories of persecution at family gatherings. So when Gregory speaks of the "momentary experience of suffering," he speaks from a family history that gave witness to God's faithfulness.*

require assistance, yet the reward is the same for everyone mentioned. He receives into heaven the spiritually impoverished and those who were persecuted for his sake, as well as those who show kindness to their neighbor. How do we account for these differences? Our answer: they are all connected with each other because they all come together in the same goal. In regards to poverty, it does not take much to alleviate poverty, and love of the poor is congruent with poverty. In any case, I think the best way to proceed is to first investigate the passage under consideration and then, once we establish its meaning, find a solution to the questions raised.

"Blessed are those who are persecuted for the sake of justice." Why are they persecuted? And by whom? The first thing that comes to mind is the martyrs and the image of the faithful running to win the prize in Christ Jesus. In both instances, pursuit is the key idea. Pursuit may mean both an act of chasing and an act of striving. In the case of a sprinter, following both definitions, it implies the goal of the sprinter is to be fast and, even more importantly, to win. The point being that a sprinter cannot be declared the winner unless she leaves her competition in the dust. Accordingly, the faithful person who runs toward the "the prize for which God has called me heavenward in Christ Jesus" (Phil 3:14 NIV) and the person who is pursued by the enemy, that is, the martyr persecuted on account of the prize, have someone behind them. The former has his competition behind him, and the latter is followed by his persecutor.

Of course, this refers to the persons who complete the course of martyrdom and are hotly pursued in the games of faith but are not overcome. To these contestants, it seems that the Lord holds out this eighth and highest blessing like a gold medal. For there is no higher blessing than to suffer for the sake of our Lord. Why? Because being hounded by evil becomes the motivation for grabbing hold of the good life. To sever your connection from evil is the ground floor for growth into the really Real, the Reality above all reality, that is, the Lord God himself, who is the highest aspiration of the person hounded by persecution. As a result, it is reasonable to say that this person is truly blessed because he uses evil as a means to attain the really Real. You see, life is lived between the boundaries of good and evil. And just as the person who gives up on the awe-inspiring hope of the really Real sinks into despair, so the one who is alienated from the sleaze of sin identifies himself with justice and integrity.

It is important to remember, especially in the instance of the martyrs, looks are deceiving. On the outside the pursuit of the martyrs by evil tyrants is by all accounts distressing, but the final chapter of their story goes beyond our wildest dreams of blessing. I think it might be helpful to provide a few more illustrations to help us dig a little deeper into the meaning of the passage. We all know that it is more difficult to hang with people who scheme against us versus people who look out for our best interest. Yet, we do have some examples available in Scripture that show how hurtful ordeals later become the source for happiness, even in this life. A good example of what I'm saying is the story of Joseph, who was sold by his brothers into slavery (see Genesis 37). His own flesh and blood conspired against him and forced him to leave the care of his family by selling him off. But it was out of their conniving that he later became their ruler. In fact, it is possible to say that he wouldn't have achieved such an honor if their envy had not paved his way to the kingdom. Now, if a seer of the future had come along and told Joseph, "Don't worry! These hurtful plots against you will be a blessing to you," do you think, living through the painful circumstances of his enslavement, he would have found these words comforting? Or credible? What is the likelihood that he could even consider that the wicked intent of his brothers would result in a happy ending? And so it was in the age of the martyrs: the painful reality of persecution made it difficult for those more captured by worldly values to receive the hope of the kingdom that came through those painful circumstances. Yet, the Lord, who knows the frailty of our makeup, announces beforehand to those weaker the goal of the contest so that they may more easily defeat the momentary experience of suffering.

This is why Stephen celebrated as he was surrounded and stoned. His body readily received the stones as if they were gentle drops of dew. He responded by blessing his murderers, praying that their sin would not be held against them. He could respond this way because he had both heard the promise and recognized that his hope was becoming real in what was happening to him. He was told beforehand that those persecuted for the Lord's sake would come into the kingdom of heaven, and then he saw what he expected in his experience of suffering. It was while running the race by his confession that he was shown his hope—the heavens opened and God's glory looked down on the sprinter's contest from his heavenly residence, and Stephen in his great effort bore witness to the Lord. The standing position of Jesus, the contest's director, provides a useful illustration of the assistance that the Lord gives to the contestant. From this illustration we should learn that the same person who directs the contest also supports his own players against their opponents. What could be more blessed than to be the one persecuted for the Lord's sake when he discovers that the contest's director is struggling on his behalf?

Let's be frank, it is not easy, and perhaps impossible, for a person to prefer the unseen good above the delicacies of life that we are able to see, such that they willingly choose to be kicked out of their home or cut off from their spouse and children, siblings, parents and friends, and the good things of life, unless their Lord worked for the good of those who have been called according to his purpose. For, as Paul wrote, "those God foreknew he also predestined, . . . those he called, he also justified . . . [and] glorified" (see Rom 8:29-30 NIV). The soul through the body becomes psychologically attached to the things that are pleasurable. It is through the eyes that we take pleasure in things of beauty. It is through the ears that we are attracted to pleasant-sounding music. Through smell, taste and touch, we are affected by the attachment naturally formed by each. These attachments formed are so strong it becomes difficult to turn our backs to them. In fact, over time we grow together with these attachments much like a turtle or a snail is attached to its shell. And like the snail, we slowly drag around these attachments gained over a lifetime. Weighed down by these burdens, the soul is easily caught by its persecutors, giving in to threats of confiscation of property or other objects valued in this life, and as a result, rolling over to the demands of their oppressor.

But when the Word of God, which, as the apostle writes, "is sharp as a surgeon's scalpel, cutting through everything" (Heb 4:12), pierces the person who has made a genuine faith commitment to Christ, he severs these unhealthy attachments from the inner person, disrupting the shackles of habit. And then that person becomes like a long-distance runner, throwing off unhealthy attachments bonded to the soul, and with his load lightened he kicks into high gear to make his way through the course guided by the course designer. No longer focused on what is behind, he turns his attention to what is ahead. He doesn't entertain second thoughts about abandoned pleasures but presses forward to what's really important. He feels no remorse over the loss of worldly amusements but is enlivened by securing the heavenly. As a result, he willing receives every method of torture as a means that will help him to grab hold of the joy he desires. He accepts fire as a means for burning off impurities, the sword as a means to dislodge the mind from destructive attachments. All techniques devised to inflict pain are willingly received as a remedy to the toxicity of pleasure. It is like someone overcome with nausea who drinks a mixture of vinegar and water to relieve his or her symptoms.

In the same way, a person facing persecution turns to God and accepts the wave of agony as a means to check the allure of pleasure. A person in pain cannot enjoy pleasure. And so, as sin entered into human experience through pleasure, so is it removed by the opposite. Those therefore who persecute the faithful for confessing the Lord, devising the most heinous methods of torture, inadvertently provided a cure to those souls through suffering—healing the infection of pleasure by the application of pain. So Paul accepts the cross, James the sword, Stephen the rocks, and the blessed Peter is crucified upside down. After the apostolic period, contestants for the faith suffered many forms of torture: tossed into pits with beasts, set on fire, frozen, sides flayed, nails ringing the head, eyes gouged, fingers cut off, limbs pulled apart from their body, starved to death. All these and similar tortures the saints joyfully embraced as a means to be cleansed from sin, so that no residue of pleasure left its mark on the heart. For the severity of the painful experience wiped out any stain pleasure left on the soul.

"Blessed," therefore, "are those who are persecuted for my sake." Let's look at this from another angle, similar to someone personifying health, who says, "Blessed are those freed from disease for my sake, because being cut off from disease makes ready those who were once bedridden to reside with me." Or hear the voice of life, which proclaims the blessing, "Blessed are those who have been persecuted by death for my sake." Or if light were to say, "Blessed are those who are persecuted by darkness for my sake." The same thing might be said of justice, holiness, incorruption, goodness, or anything else we can bring to mind in regards to the virtuous life. It is not too farfetched to imagine the Lord saying to you, "Blessed is the person who steers clear of everything destructive—corruption, darkness, sin, injustice, covetousness, and anything and everything that opposes the good in thought, word and deed." Why? Because to be cut off from evil means to be on the side of goodness. As the Lord says, "Anyone who chooses a life of sin is trapped in a dead-end life and is, in fact, a slave" (Jn 8:34). Therefore, any person who is trapped in a dead-end life and leaves it behind gains their freedom.

Now the highest form of freedom is self-determination. The king, in the ancient world, represents the highest form of self-determination in society because no one tells the king what to do. It follows that if a person is freed from sin, he or she is self-determining; and if the nature of kingship is to be sovereign and second to no one, then the person who is persecuted by evil is blessed because persecution of this kind secures for him or her the status of royalty.

So, brothers and sisters, do not be depressed at losing the things of this life. For people who find themselves in these circumstances also find themselves in the palaces of heaven. Rational beings, like us, are made to live in one of two realms— earth or heaven. The place made for those in the flesh is earth, whereas heaven is for the incorporeal. We are made in such a way that we are required to live in one or the other. And unless we were hounded away from earth we would remain here. But if we depart from here we gain a new home in heaven. Are you beginning to get a handle on where the beatitude leads, since through visible suffering such a great good is achieved? The apostle shows that he got it when he wrote, "At the time, discipline isn't much fun. It always feels like it's going against the grain. Later, of course, it pays off handsomely, for it's the well-trained who find themselves mature in their relationship with God" (Heb 12:11).

Hardship is the investment that will yield the hoped-for returns. Therefore, for the sake of this high return, let us make the investment. Let us suffer being pursued so that we may run. And if running, let us not run for running's sake but keeping our eye on the goal "where God is beckoning [us] onward" (Phil 3:14), and let us run so that we may win. What is the winner's prize? I'm convinced that it is nothing other than the Lord Jesus himself. He is the course designer, race official and the prize for those who win. He is the executor of the inheritance, and he himself is the inheritance. He makes you rich, and he is the riches. He leads you to the treasure, and he is himself the treasure. He entices you to desire the pearl of great price and makes it available for purchase. So let us sell off the things that we have in order to purchase what we don't have. So let's not get down if we are persecuted, because by being cut off from earthly honors, we are pushed toward the heavenly Good. For Jesus has promised that those who have been persecuted for his sake will be blessed, for theirs is the kingdom of the heavens, by the grace of our Lord Jesus Christ, to whom be glory and power forever and ever. Amen.

# Discussion Questions

1. Gregory argues that the goal of the really good life is likeness to God. What does it mean to be "like" God? Is likeness to God achievable in this life? Why or why not?

2. Gregory makes humility the gateway to life of spiritual maturity and happiness. How do you define humility?

3. "The proud learn only from experience—the wise learn from the experience of others." How do you react to this statement?

1. In life and nature there is tendency toward evil that can quickly gain momentum if given the chance. In this context Gregory defines meekness as the gentle refusal to stoke the flames of evil. Who are the meek? "The meek are persons who gently and quietly refuse to encourage or participate in evil." What do you think of this definition of "the meek"?

2. Does God require us to be free from conflicting emotions? If not, what does he expect of us?

3. What "soul cure" does Gregory suggest for those easily swept away by their impulses?

◆SERMON 3

1. What are the different meanings that Gregory assigns to mourning?

2. In life, we develop spiritual calluses sometimes through neglect and other times because of difficult circumstances. The result of these calluses is that we become less sensitive to God's love and affection in our lives. What is the remedy that God has provided for this condition? How do we make this remedy a part of our daily life?

3. Gregory says Jesus called mourning blessed not for its own sake but because of what it attracts—comfort? Pain and suffering then become an opportunity to experience the comfort of God. How would this perspective change (or not) your experience of painful circumstances?

◆SERMON 4

1. What is justice? How do Gregory's definitions of justice compare with your definition(s)?

2. What does it mean to hunger for stones? What does it mean to hunger for justice that Jesus desires?

3. Gregory makes this point: Don't waste your energy pursuing things that will ultimately end in nothing. It is simply foolhardy to make these your life's ambition. It is like someone trying to catch their shadow. They can pursue it forever but it will always elude their grasp. A wiser course of action would be to direct your attention to objects which if pursued would be made your own. What are the "shadows" you are pursuing in your life?

4. According to Gregory, why are those who hunger for the justice of God called blessed?

## ◆SERMON 5

1. Who is the compassionate person?
2. What does Gregory mean when he states that we should have compassion on our souls?
3. How would this act of compassion impact your soul?
4. Gregory says people pronounce judgment on themselves by how they treat each other. What do you think?
5. How does our compassion in this life impact the afterlife?

## ◆SERMON 6

1. As Gregory meditated on this beatitude he described his experience as standing on a cliff overlooking an ocean of infinite depth. What do you think he means?
2. Jesus promises that the pure in heart will see God, yet Scripture also teaches that no one can see God and live. Are these teachings contradictory? If not, how do you resolve this tension?
3. How do we see God in this life?
4. How do we become pure in heart?

## ◆SERMON 7

1. Why is it important for spiritual formation to come to terms with the fact that what we know about God is like a drop of rain in an ocean?
2. Gregory makes the case for the importance of peace within a country and among nations. If this is so, what is our responsibility to promote peace in our community, nation and world?
3. What does it mean to you to be a peacemaker?

## ◆SERMON 8

1. Gregory argues that the hard work of the virtuous life requires that we look beyond our earthly circumstances to our future life in God's kingdom. If this is true, what we believe about the afterlife is relevant to how we live today. What do you believe about heaven? How does this understanding of heaven influence how you live today?

2. What stories do we tell when our friends and family gather? The faith of Gregory's grandmother Macrina, refined by persecution, became the seedbed of Christian faithfulness for later generations of her family. Take some time today and remember the stories of faith from your family tree. Thank God for these previous generations. Reflect: What is the spiritual legacy you would like to leave future generations?

3. Though not stated explicitly it seems that Gregory is making the case that courage is essential to spiritual maturity. What undermines courage? What promotes courage?

**formatio**
TRADITION. EXPERIENCE.
TRANSFORMATION.

Formatio books from InterVarsity Press follow the rich tradition of the church in the journey of spiritual formation. These books are not merely about being informed, but about being transformed by Christ and conformed to his image. Formatio stands in InterVarsity Press's evangelical publishing tradition by integrating God's Word with spiritual practice and by prompting readers to move from inward change to outward witness. InterVarsity Press uses the chambered nautilus for Formatio, a symbol of spiritual formation because of its continual spiral journey outward as it moves from its center. We believe that each of us is made with a deep desire to be in God's presence. Formatio books help us to fulfill our deepest desires and to become our true selves in light of God's grace.